INSTRUCTOR'S MANUAL

to accompany

Harvey/Allard
UNDERSTANDING DIVERSITY
READINGS, CASES, AND EXERCISES

Carol P. Harvey
Assumption College

M. June Allard
Worcester State College

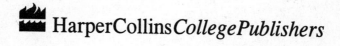 HarperCollins*CollegePublishers*

Instructor's Manual to accompany Harvey/Allard, Understanding Diversity: Readings, Cases and Exercises

Copyright © 1995 HarperCollins*College Publishers*

ISBN: 0-673-55832-0

94 95 96 97 98 9 8 7 6 5 4 3 2 1

Table of Contents

SECTION I
Teaching a Course in Diversity

Introduction

There are many approaches to teaching about diversity. *Understanding Diversity: Readings, Cases and Exercises* was designed to provide a flexible anthology and source of experiential material that can be used by the instructor in college classes or workshops related to issues of diversity in business, education, the social sciences, etc. Although this book can be used alone for a course or seminar on workforce diversity, it can also be used as a supplement to a theoretical text in any in discipline.

Teaching about diversity is still in a developmental stage. Unlike organizational behavior or management, there is not a well researched, widely accepted theoretical base. However, since much work has been done on the topic of understanding differences in the social sciences, we have included material from these disciplines that we think contributes to broadening students' understanding of these diverse issues.

Because of the complexity of the subject, few writers can be knowledgeable about all aspects of diversity. Consequently, we have selected material written from many different perspectives. Instructors are encouraged to utilize this material in any way that meets the needs of their class and their own particular theoretical perspective.

The idea for this book came from the frustrating experience of being unable to find a suitable book for a managing diversity class. After consulting with many other instructors and examining the syllabi they so generously shared, we came to the conclusion that most college teachers feel the same way. Most are trying to use a trade book on diversity and are supplementing it with numerous handouts, usually articles, but sometimes when they can find them cases and exercises as well. The inconvenience of this patchwork system and the difficulties of obtaining copyright permissions make it time consuming for the instructor and somewhat disjointed and unwieldy for the students.

These conclusions were also supported by feedback from students. They often complained about the number of handouts and a lack of continuity in the reading material. Students also told us that experientially based material was one of the most effective pieces of their learning experience and they requested more of it.

Finding and selecting appropriate material was an involved process. A dozen or so of the readings we have included here are very popular and appear on most of the syllabi that we consulted. This text provides a convenient method for legally using this material. In addition, we sought out other works to fill in the gaps and give coverage to neglected areas. We have also included a large number of pieces that have never been published before and were either written specifically for this book or are adaptations of material developed by experienced instructors and consultants for their own classroom or training use.

The text is divided into five chapters and the first three chapters are organized from a macro to a micro perspective. We have found that beginning with the larger issues of difference in society (Chapter I) and progressing to organizations (Chapter II) and then to specific types of diverse groups (Chapter III) works well with our classes. This approach is less threatening to the students in the majority culture who may have difficulty comprehending why understanding diversity is even an issue. In addition, it works well with students from minority cultures who feel less pressure to serve as the spokesperson for their particular groups when difference is first considered from a broader perspective. The macro to micro approach allows students to begin their examination of issues of difference from the vantage point that we are all different in some ways, yet similar in others.

However, to provide maximum flexibility for the needs of your class, and your particular theoretical perspective, it is not necessary to follow the order of this book, if it does not fit your approach. Nor is it necessary to assign all of the readings. Choose what will work for your class.

Chapter IV is designed to bring enhanced awareness and increased knowledge of diversity to each student by providing him/her with opportunities to apply theory to actual practice through the use of case analysis. Chapter V provides a wide selection of experiential material designed to increase students awareness and knowledge of differences by giving them the opportunity to participate more actively in their own learning process.

We have deliberately refrained from grouping readings, cases and exercises together to allow the instructor maximum flexibility. For your convenience, topic matrices and suggested syllabi are provided in this manual. Because classes are so different - large and small, diverse and homogeneous, short and long in length, etc., we have tried to provide the instructor with experiential material to meet needs of a wide range of situations.

The text is supported by this instructor's manual which contains suggestions for organizing and teaching classes about diversity, key points and answers to all discussion questions, detailed instructions for administering the exercises, and a list of additional resources. Whether you teach a specific course about diversity or use this book to integrate diversity issues into other courses, understand that you are on the cutting edge of this field. We welcome correspondence from instructors that informs us how you use this material and offers additional suggestions.

Carol P. Harvey, Ed.D.
Associate Professor
Department of Business Studies
Assumption College
500 Salisbury St.
Worcester, MA 01615-0005

M. June Allard, Ph.D.
Professor
Department of Psychology
Worcester State College
486 Chandler Street
Worcester, MA 01602-2597

Organization of the Instructor's Manual

This manual is designed to provide you with assistance in teaching your course and contains the following:

SECTION I
- General overview to teaching about diversity

- A reprint of Kate Kirkham's article, *Teaching About Diversity: Navigating the Emotional Undercurrents*

- Topic matrices for selecting cases, readings and exercises - Suggested topic outlines for 11 and 14 week semesters

SECTION II
- Key points and answers to discussion questions for all of the readings from Chapters I, II, and III of the text

SECTION III
- Instruction notes, answers to discussion questions, and updates where available for the cases from Chapter IV of the text

SECTION IV
- Detailed instructions for administering all of the exercises found in Chapter V of the text

SECTION V
- Selected bibliography of current materials on diversity: books, videos, newsletter etc.

Teaching About Issues of Diversity: *Practical Considerations*

This section is designed to provide some practical suggestions, and ideas for teaching about diversity. We begin with a consideration of some of the nitty gritty teaching details that we have learned both through experience and the sharing of ideas with colleagues. This is followed by an important article by Kate Kirkham, Teaching About Diversity: Navigating the Emotional Undercurrents. We have reprinted Kirkham's article in the instructor's manual for your benefit because we believe that anyone teaching about diversity needs to be prepared for the strong feelings and emotional reactions that this topic can raise in the classroom. This section concludes with sample course outlines and matrices for the readings, cases and exercises.

Backlash

Not only may backlash occur in your classes, in fact it is to be expected. Diversity is an emotional issue that often involves deeply held values. When these beliefs are examined and challenged, defensive behavior often results. It is for this reason that we have included the Kirkham article in the instructor's manual.

Guest Speakers

This is one of the most valuable ways to teach students about diversity. We have found good speakers by calling up diverse people featured in newspaper articles and inviting them to class, and by asking business contacts or anyone who will listen to us for suggestions. It is best to prepare your speakers by explaining the focus of your course and by sending him/her a copy of the syllabus. The candor of the speakers has surprised us. Most are quite willing to talk about private issues and feelings.

Student Journals

Many of the courses that involve issues of diversity use journal writing as an integral part of the course. Through journals students can freely express ideas that they may not feel comfortable expressing in the classroom. Discussion questions from the readings can be assigned as journal entries, you can formulate your own questions, or you can simply ask students to write down their reactions and feelings about a particular reading, exercise, or speaker. A particularly interesting article on journal writing is "Management Class Journals" by Dennis R. Laker from *The Organizational Behavior Teaching Review*, (1988-89), vol. XIV, 3, 72-78.

Some instructors use journals as the basis for a final paper. Students can be asked to analyze their journals for patterns, or assess changes in their attitudes and feelings about diversity over the course of the semester.

Out of Class Assignments

It has been our experience that few professors administer formal in class tests in this subject but some do assign thoughtful questions often based on the readings as take home type final exams. It is more common to assign papers written around such topics as:

Experiencing Being Different: assign students to write a report on what it is like to be a true minority by having them experience it first hand (i.e. wearing a gay rights T shirt and walking down the street hand in hand with someone of the same sex, white students attending a service at a predominantly black church, males attending a meeting that they expect to be predominantly attended by females, going shopping in a wheelchair, etc.

Interviews: have students interview people in the workforce who have experience around issues of diversity to learn more about the realities of difference. Parents, friends, and human resource managers are often good sources for students to contact to find the highest ranking woman in an organization, an openly gay or lesbian employee, a physically challenged employee, the only racial minority on a board of trustees, etc.

Television, Films, and Books: Students are highly influenced by the media. Assign a paper or presentation based on application of the theoretical material from this course on topics such as stereotyping, race, gender etc., to be applied to the content of television programs, commercials, etc.

Students can be assigned or choose films, and popular books such as *Noble House, The Joy Luck Club, Like Water for Chocolate, The Woman's Room, Do the Right Thing*, etc., to relate to the theory of the course.

Create an Exercise: from this text is an ideal group and/or final assignment that students really enjoy doing.

Team Teaching

This system is highly recommended if your institution will support it. Having diverse individuals teach the course is the ideal because of the variety of perspectives that they bring into the classroom. It also helps to decrease the backlash of students thinking that an individual instructor, especially if he or she is diverse, has a personal agenda.

Class Competition

A diversity class, like the workplace, is enriched by having students of different races, genders, sexual orientations, and physical abilities. However, the instructor has to be careful to resist the tendency to expect these students to represent and speak for their aspect of diversity. This tends to provoke an "us" vs "them" mentality. For in-class exercises and group projects try to integrate groups in terms of difference unless other directions are given in the instructions. Students can learn a lot from working on a diverse team.

If your class is somewhat homogeneous, suggestions are given in the instructor's directions for exercises that are particularly useful for in the more visibly homogeneous classes.

Teaching About Diversity: *Navigating the Emotional Undercurrents**

Kate Kirkham
Brigham Young University

Different topics in organizational behavior - power, motivation, the utility of small groups - generate different but reasonably predictable relations in class discussions. However, nothing has proven more predictable than the reactions created by introducing race and gender topics into the curriculum. Any aspect (racism, sex role stereotyping, child care) produces emotionally charged statements that seem to ricochet in the discussion.

From my teaching, research and consulting practice, I have learned that these emotional undercurrents in race and gender related discussions can be "charted." Knowing more about the underlying emotions doesn't prevent them from being a part of the classroom, but increases the likelihood of learning when and how to surface them in a discussion. This article identifies a source of the emotional intensity and explores diagnostic questions useful in understanding the emotional dimensions of race and gender topics.

Sources of Emotions

Emotional intensity is a part of teaching about race and gender topics in any learning situation whether it is the traditional graduate or undergraduate classroom, a corporate training session or community workshop. In my experience, age, occupation or education of those present are not consistent predictors of how emotional the discussion will be. Neither does the numerical distribution of men, women and/or racially different individuals in a discussion totally explain the emotions. While emotional intensity is often associated with a recent racist/sexist incident in the community or organizational lives of the participants, such incidents determine how the emotions will surface and not the underlying presence or absence of emotional tensions in race and gender discussions.

What are the sources of emotions? My colleagues and classroom participants can quickly identify the emotions that come from two clear sources: comments that are perceived as either *advocating* or *resisting* certain core beliefs or experiences. Wanting someone else to change and not wanting to be someone's "change target" do contribute to the ebb and flow of emotions. And, my awareness of how those advocating and resisting certain views affects a group discussion, has provided some help in effectively navigating race and gender topics. However, more recently, "advocate" and "resistor" have proven to be insufficient labels for the complexity of issues surrounding race and gender.

My work with both student and other groups indicates that the best predictor of emotions underlying a race and/or gender discussion is the criteria participants are using to determine the legitimacy of the topic. Individuals have implicit assumptions as criteria for their view of the legitimacy of race and gender issues in today's society and, therefore, what is "fair" for them and others in a discussion. For example, the contributions of an individual who thinks that he/she or the topic are being treated unfairly are predictably going to be emotionally charged. The criteria individuals use for assessing legitimacy are not easily summarized under "advocating" or "resisting" change. Ferreting out the core assumptions about legitimacy enables the emotional intensity to be more richly explored for all involved in discussion.

A brief comparison to other OB topics helps illustrate this relationship between legitimacy and emotional intensity. I find a wide range of student emotional responses to the *dynamics* of political behavior in organizations; but universal agreement that it is a legitimate *area of study* in the field of organizational behavior. Leadership is seen as a critical area of legitimate concern for all organizational members, even those who won't be CEOs. However, in many discussions the criteria governing *baseline* legitimacy of a race and gender topic are often not shared by participants in a discussion. What one person thinks is a discussion of how to address a specific racial incident in a

---

*Reprinted with permission from The Organizational Behavior Teaching Review, Vol. XII, 4, 1988-1989, Sage Publications, Inc.

company may be for someone else additional evidence that others don't understand the real problems. Having access to this undercurrent of assumptions and strong feelings about the legitimacy of race and gender issues is essential.

Diagnostic Guides

Three basic diagnostic questions enable individuals to surface their underlying assumptions about the legitimacy of race and gender topics and provides us, as instructors, with access to the core emotions that may be present in a discussion.

(1) Who really is racist or sexist?

(2) What constitutes *tangible* proof of race/gender issues?

(3) What is the real problem and how big a problem is "it"?

Before discussing each of these questions, there are two observations important for the use of the diagnostic questions themselves:

(1) Because two students are equally emotionally demonstrative doesn't mean that the source of their emotions is similar. And, whether a student is relatively quiet or talkative in a classroom isn't the best indicator of his/her ability to articulate either the criteria they are using or emotions associated with it. Both the quiet person who really can clearly articulate issues and the very verbal one who isn't clarifying much are as present in race and gender discussions as in others. But, we may make different assumptions about participation when the topic is race and gender.

(2) The race and gender of individuals often does make a difference both in how they respond to issues and how they are seen by others. In teaching about diversity, this has meant I must watch for *similarities* for members of a group that accumulate without resorting to *stereotypes* about individuals because they are a member of a racial or gender group. My experience is that majority group members in the U.S., whites and males, frequently have different assumptions underlying their emotional exploration of these three questions than do most members of other groups. I do not expect all racial or gender-like individuals to think alike. But, there are similarities in the underlying assumptions that members of a racial or gender group bring to a discussion.

One such similarity is that many majority group members do not move quickly or comfortably back and forth between their *individual* identity and their identity *as a member* of a racial or gender group in this society. If they do think of themselves as a member of a group, it is often associated with negative emotions: feeling stereotyped or threatened, etc. Therefore, majority group members may enter a discussion less prepared to sort out what is being said about the behavior of *numbers of whites (or men) as experienced by others* and the impact of their *own individual behavior*. When I am working with minorities and white women they report more familiarity in examining the experiences of the "many" as well as their own unique and individually-based experiences. Most can also articulate both the positive and negative emotions associated with their racial or gender identity. Assumptions about individual and group identity involve very different emotions in race and gender discussions.

Who is Racist/Sexist?

The three questions are linked and will not surface in a neat, orderly way in a discussion, but, they can be identified. Surfacing assumptions about who *really* is racist or sexist (in an organization or in society) is of fundamental importance in teaching about diversity. Often student emotions surrounding this question are the touchstone for the other two questions.

10

When asked to respond to the question of who *really* is racist and/or sexist, many majority group individuals, in my research and teaching experience, assume: "If I didn't intend something as racist or sexist then it is not racist/sexist." In other words, the general criteria they use in testing racism/sexism is an overpersonalized one. They believe that personal motive determines the presence of racism or sexism in interactions.

An example of this assumption is present in the pattern of reactions of a majority group member in a graduate OB course during a discussion of racism and sexism in the workplace. Every comment made by a woman or minority student in the class was responded to by him (as soon as he had a chance) as if they had been directing their comments to him personally therefore indicting his intentions. He resented this and kept saying so with increasing emotional intensity. With some assistance, he identified the core reason for his reactions. He became aware that he was using what he thought was intended as the only legitimate criteria. If the point someone was making did not fit what he thought was intended in an example, then it was not an example of racism or sexism. Because he was emotionally defending what he thought were personal and unfair accusations, he could not broaden his understanding of racism and sexism. Once he realized that others were using criteria that included intended *and* unintended outcomes of behavior, he could better understand their examples.

An additional insight came from the above class discussion and indicates the usefulness of surfacing underlying assumptions that trigger emotions in a discussion. Many of the majority group members, who had been quick to label a minority group member as over-sensitive became more aware of how their own version of over-sensitivity was showing up with just as much emotional conviction behind it.

Ironically, the most bigoted or chauvinistic majority group member is sometimes the least likely to over-personalize in the way I have just described. The class member whose opinions are very entrenched may not be affected at all by discussion. The more moderate or naive or frustrated students who are more vocal in a discussion can buffer attention to the most opinionated person. In a recent class, one usually talkative student, whose prior comments outside of the class had indicated to some that he had strong stereotypes about women, had not been participating and was finally asked for his reactions to the current discussion of gender issues. He indicated that it had not bothered him at all because he felt it was a waste of time to be discussing these issues in the course anyway. Perhaps this majority group member represents those with the most tenacious personal criteria: I do not intend to examine my views.

The societal context of race and gender issues in this country affects our ability to navigate these underlying emotions in classroom discussions, especially exploring the different assumptions about who really is racist/sexist. In fact, the accessibility of the assumptions is a good barometer of the legitimacy generated by the larger political/ economic climate outside the classroom. A decade ago, the most bigoted persons spoke out. Often in defending their views they claimed an absent but interested constituency through expressions such as "lots of us believe..."or "this is the way things are supposed to be, we have always..." Later the "messages" from society conveyed by political and legal means suggested to many that stereotypic views were no longer appropriate. My experience during this time was that majority group members who became more involved with race and gender issues reported in their discussions that the messages had generated either (1) a reluctant awareness that the issues represented changes they would have to learn to live with or (2) a genuine interest but lack of experience or awareness with either racism or sexism.

Teaching about race and gender issues is still affected by the larger societal context. Students of diversity now describe messages from society that support the core assumption by many majority group members that individual intention is a sufficient criteria in determining who or what is racist/sexist. These include: (1) statements which represent the view "we've dealt with the civil rights issues;" (2) discrimination cases which require proof of intention and personal discrimination, rather than existence of certain conditions for affected groups and, (3) a decreasing attention in the dominant media to the severity of race and gender group issues, while highlighting the success of individuals. These messages and their role in legitimizing certain assumptions must be explored in a discussion of race and gender issues and the emotional implications surfaced.

Majority and minority participants in a discussion also have different assumptions about what constitutes sufficient proof of the existence of discrimination, racism or sexism. Once participants in a discussion realize that intention is not the only criteria, they can better discern that men and women working in the same organization may experience the *outcome* of company practices differently because of their gender. Also, white and black co-workers may have different perceptions of the affect of behaviors in a meeting. A man may focus on the outcome of one example and fail to find sufficient evidence of sexism while the woman experiences the one example as symptomatic of the experience of being different in a sexist organization.

Individual majority group members do not hear or see in their day-to-day interactions the very examples the minority person offers as proof of the existence of racism or sexism. Certainly majority group members do not pass on stories to each other about what they did to contribute to sexism in their organizations. The research on sexual harassment, for example, has recorded that it is a few of the men who do most of the harassing. The problem is that the behaviors of many of the men may not make it obvious who is the one who will later harass. Several men may "enjoy" a sexist joke but only one may continue his "enjoyment" of sexism by harassing women he works with in the organization. However, the men that allow the joke, all "look" like potential harassers. The men may individually (i.e., personally) dismiss or tolerate the joking without seeing how it fuels the one or two men who will continue to bring inappropriate sexual conduct into the workplace. The women who hear or hear about the joking may be weary of all those who allowed it. The men who allow joking, language or inappropriate discussion of women's appearance to occur at one point in time will not be present later when the behavior of other men becomes even more severely sexist.

Participants in race and gender discussions might also assume that only the most severe examples constitute real proof of a problem. So, if someone can't produce the "Archie Bunker" incident, then those suggesting that racism exists are discounted or accused of exaggerating the issues for today's workforce. But it is the accumulated impact of subtle expressions of racism and sexism that is of the most severe "incident."

Majority group members are faced with some additional problems in both generating or hearing several examples that would provide more proof. If a majority group member isn't convinced yet of the existence of a problem of discrimination or managing diversity and more data are offered, that additional data can be experienced as complaining. This is especially true if the person offering the example ends up getting the attention rather than the example itself: a man says "I just don't understand" when asked about discrimination in his department; a woman then offers an example or two and he responds: "Is that it?" She offers a few more examples before he says in essence, "If you're so bothered by all this why are you working here?" Even though her response back is that she is not personally complaining but attempting to inform him about the ever-present experience of being different, the discussion now shifts to her oversensitivity rather than a discussion of his ability to explore these examples or discuss differences in general.

Not only are these additional data seen as complaining but it is difficult for a majority group member to listen to a series of examples without beginning to feel implicated and, therefore, more emotionally defensive as indicated in the earlier example of how certain assumptions can result in overpersonalizing a discussion of the issues. However, if the majority group members have been prepared for this interaction, they then can hear any number of examples and think "I don't want to be identified with racism/sexism, so it is in my self interest to learn more about it so that my behavior is more non-racist/sexist." This posture invites more dialogue than the retorts such as "Hey, you can't say that about all whites (or men)" or "You haven't seen me do that." It is important to examine assumptions about what constitutes proof of a problem and differences which may exist for majority and minority group members.

All this is not to say that every example of racism or sexism offered in a discussion is always racist or sexist. Poor communication skills can be perceived as racist, for example, or a man questioning a woman's ability to do a job may have nothing to do with her gender. What is evident is that the legitimacy of some of the examples offered as proof are more easily challenged than the behaviors of majority group members as they react to or discuss the examples.

What Really is the Problem and How Big a Problem is It?

In addition to the emotion generated by assumptions about one's personal intentions and the proof required, there are often fundamental differences in how the problem is defined. Some people assume that the real problem is the presence or absence of women and minorities. Others may believe that the real problem is the behavior of the different person: not aggressive enough or "qualified." Still others assume it is the policies of an organization or its practices that favor one group at the expense of another.

Perhaps the most emotional aspect of defining the problem is in examining the perceptions held by racially different women and men about the magnitude of the problem for today's workforce. If the assumptions operating about the definition and magnitude of the problem are not explored, then talking about solutions will deteriorate because suggestions made by some based on one definition will not be viewed as legitimate by someone else. Problem and solution simply will not match.

In some discussions about the definition of the problem, the fundamental assumption will center on who really has the right to define the problem. Defining a problem is a form of power. Difference, diversity and discrimination are all embedded in power relationships in most organizations. In fact, the core assumptions discussed earlier are often emotionally anchored in one's view of who is in charge and why. Surfacing the criteria individuals are using to define the problem is essential in planning for change.

Classroom Interventions

In teaching about diversity there are many ways to generate examining assumptions of both majority and minority group members - within and between groups. Each of the following ways can make a contribution to the challenges of exploring diversity and navigating the underlying emotions.

(1) Present Agree/Disagree Statements. List statements that have a range of ambiguity in them, then provide small group discussion time. Examples of statements that can help surface the legitimacy of issues and the emotions involved are:

(1) Women are as capable and able as men in organizations to hold upper level management positions.

(2) One's race or gender is a part of the first impression a person makes in an organization.

(3) I can identify prejudicial behaviors in others.

(4) Current practices in organizations limit advancement for minority women and men.

(2) Assign Students to Interview other Students who are racially different from and racially like the interviewer. Provide suggestions for questions such as: What is it like to be _____ on this campus? (Fill in the blank with either a race, culture, or gender identity); or, Do you think your race (gender) affects how others interact with you?

(3) Assist Students in Getting an Historical Perspective. First, utilize reading from different cases, especially those that convey the personal experience of individuals alive during another period. Second, assign or prepare an historical survey of major business journals for illustrations or articles with race/gender implications. It would also be possible to interview individuals from a different generation than those in the class.

(4) Creatively Utilize the Resources in Different Materials such as video, news programs, talk shows and films.

(5) Create Visions of Integrated Society or Organizations. Explore perceptions of how problems are being defined, what constitutes proof and perceptions of how committed racially different women and men are to achieving the vision.

Sample Course Outline for 11 Week Semester

Week	Topics	Readings; Cases	Exercises
1	Introduction to Diversity	"On Culture and Diversity," Miner & Sowell	Allard (I Am...) Bromberg & Harvey
2	Understanding Diversity/Stereotypes	Sawin Gould & White	Bowman
3	Overview of Workforce Diversity/Conflict	"On Organizations & Diversity," R. R. Thomas, Parker	Harvey or Hunt (Workforce I.Q.)
4	EEO/AA/Valuing Diversity	Kubasek & Giapetro, Nazario Feltes et al, Case: Crowner & Prychiak	Harvey (Is This Sexual Harassment)
5	Understandig Gender Issues	"On Dimensions of Diversity" Kanter, Case: Harvey (Briarwood)	Gallos
6	Understanding Gender in the Workplace (or mid-term exam)	Gallese, Billard Case: Sadd	G. Klein, Kuntsler
7	Understanding Racial/Ethnic Issues	McIntosh Case: E. Thomas or Mosler	Parker & D. Klein
8	Understanding Racial/Ethnic Issues	Rivera Case: Winfield	Thiederman, Winfield (Test of Management Knowledge), Shriberg
9	Understanding Disabilities & Age Issues	Prince Case: DiBiasio	Allard (Musical Chairs) Nkomo et al
10	Understanding Sexual Orientation Issues	Hunt Case: Howard	

Alternatives for Final Week of Class

11A	Integration of Multiple Issues of Diversity	Cox & Blake Case: Hogan	Diodati, O'Neil
11B	Class presentation of Create an Exercise (Allard) Final Assignment		
11C	Final Exam/Project		

Sample Course Outline for 14 Week Semester

Week	Topics	Readings; Cases	Exercises
1	Introduction to Diversity	"On Culture and Diversity," Miner & Sowell	Allard (I Am...) Bromberg & Harvey
2	Understanding Diversity/Stereotypes	Sawin Gould & White	Bowman
3	Overview of Workforce Diversity/Conflict	"On Organizations & Diversity," R. R. Thomas, Parker	Harvey or Hunt (Workforce I.Q.)
4	EEO/AA	Kubasek & Giapetro, Nazario Case: Crowner	Harvey (Is This Sexual Harassment)
5	Valuing Diversity/Global Issues	Butterfield, Feltes	Thiederman
6	Understandig Gender Issues	"On Dimensions of Diversity" Kanter, Case: Harvey (Briarwood)	Gallos
7	Understanding Gender in the Workplace	Gallese, Billard Case: Sadd	G. Klein, Kuntsler
8	Understanding Cultural Issues	Cox & Blake (optional: Parker/D. Klein reading)	Parker & D. Klein, Shriberg
9	Understanding Racial/Ethnic Issues	McIntosh Case: C. Thomas or Mosler	
10	Understanding Racial/Ethnic Issues	Rivera Case: Winfield	Winfield (Test of Management Knowledge)
11	Understanding Disabilities & Age Issues	Prince Case: DiBiasio	Allard (Musical Chairs) Nkomo et al
12	Understanding Sexual Orientation Issues	Hunt Case: Howard	
13	Integration of Multiple Issues of Diversity	Cox & Blake Case: Hogan	Diodati, O'Neil
14	Class presentation of Create an Exercise (Allard) Exam/Project, Final Assignment, etc.		

READINGS TOPIC MATRIX

Readings	Understanding Differences	Stereotype Prejudices	EEO/AA Legal	Change	Culture	Managing Diversity	Gender	Race/Ethnicity	Age	Physical Challenge	Sexual Orientation
Miner	X	X				X					
Sowell	X			X		X					
Sawin	X	X			X						
Gould & White	X	X					X				
Rivera	X				X	X		X			
Parker	X			X	X	X					
R.R. Thomas Jr.	X		X	X	X	X	X	X	X	X	X
Cox & Blake				X	X	X	X	X			
Kubasek & Giapetro			X	X			X	X			
Nazario			X	X		X		X			
Feltes et al	X		X		X	X	X	X			
Butterfield		X	X	X	X		X	X			
Kanter	X	X	X	X	X		X				
Gallese	X	X	X	X	X		X				
Billard	X	X	X	X	X		X				
McIntosh	X	X					X	X			
Prince	X	X	X	X	X					X	X
Hunt	X	X	X	X	X						X

CASES TOPIC MATRIX

Cases	Understanding Differences	Stereotypes Prejudices	EEO/AA Legal Issues	Change	Managing Diversity	Culture	Gender	Race/ Ethnicity	Age	Physical Challenge	Sexual Orientation
Continental Airlines	X	X	X	X	X		X				
Al the Joker	X	X	X		X						
Briarwood	X	X	X		X		X				
Freida Mae Jones	X	X	X	X	X		X	X			
The Emanuel Company	X	X		X	X			X			
General Dynamics	X	X	X	X	X	X	X	X			
Mail Management Systems	X		X	X	X		X			X	
Cracker Barrel	X	X	X	X	X						X
Mobil Oil Corporation	X		X	X	X	X	X	X			

EXERCISES TOPIC MATRIX

Exercise Title	Awareness	Knowledge	Application	Stereotypes	Gender	Race/ Ethnicity	Age	Disability	Sexual Orientation
I Am...	X								
Workforce I.Q. (U.S.)		X							
Workforce I.Q. (Canada)		X							
Exploring Diversity	X								
Increasing Multicultural Understanding		X		X					
Invisible Volleyball Game		X			X				
Women & Work		X		X	X				
Is This Sexual Harassment?			X		X				
Cultural Diversity Quiz		X			X				
Test of Management Knowledge/Navajo		X				X			
Creating Your Own Culture			X	X					
Musical Chairs	X	X	X	X				X	
The Older Worker		X		X			X		
Transcendus			X	X		X			
Gender & Participation			X	X	X	X			
The In-Basket Dilemma		X	X	X	X	X	X	X	X
Multicultural Negotiations Exercise	X	X	X	X	X				
Create an Exercise	X	X	X	X	X	X	X	X	X

SECTION II
Readings: *Key Points and Answers to Discussion Questions*

On Culture and Diversity

Body Ritual Among the Nacirema

Key Points

An anthropologist takes the role of an observer from a culture more developed than our own and describes features of our civilization in the same manner as we describe cultures we view as primitive.

- To understand culture we must be able to stand back and view our own culture as others might.

- In describing some aspects of American culture ("Nacerima" is "American" spelled backward), Miner shows that to more advanced cultures (and by extension to future generations), our culture today may well be considered primitive.

- It is important to get away from the parochial view that one's own culture is "right" or "normal" or "superior" and that other cultures are more inconsistent or strange or inferior to our own.

- We think of "primitive" cultures as practicing magic, but rarely see this element in our own culture.

- Our culture has rituals just as "primitive" cultures do.

Answers to Discussion Questions

1. What general message do you think the author was trying to convey in this description of American culture?

   - Message: The behaviors and beliefs that we take for granted look as strange to other cultures as their behaviors and beliefs do to us.

2. Why are some behaviors described as "magic"?

   - "Magic" refers to art (or arts) in which the practitioners call upon supernatural powers or have mastery of secret forces in nature. To a more advanced culture, our hygiene and medical and dental practices appear to use the powers of nature to produce desired results (such as cures and avoidance of disease).

3. Why are some behaviors described as "rituals"? Do you think this is a fair label?

   - Rituals are a code of ceremonies or rites. All cultures have rituals. To a civilization more advanced than our own, many of our hygiene and dental and medical practices would seem like rituals.

4. Does the humorous approach to our culture bother you? Do you feel that the description is belittling or sarcastic in tone?

   - Students bothered by the humorous approach and those who feel the description is belittling may not have learned to stand back and view their own culture objectively and may have difficulty in appreciating diverse perspectives on other issues.

5. Imagine you are a member of the author's culture. What kinds of stereotypes would you probably have of the American culture and its people if this reading were your only source of information?

- Promotes strange practices

- Highly developed market economy

- Very, very magic-ridden

- Not very advanced in health care and practices

- Very conscious of physical appearance

Optional Assignment

Instruct students to write about some aspect of American culture (not covered in the Miner article) in the same way as Miner does. Examples: dating patterns, child rearing, Halloween customs, educational practices, etc.

A World View of Cultural Diversity

Key Points

This reading places modern concern with cultural diversity in perspective, adding depth and a whole new dimension to the understanding of the term, by presenting an historic and international overview. A number of points are illustrated:

- The history of humankind is characterized by civilizations sharing cultural advances.

- All cultures constantly change.

- Some features of cultures are better than others; cultures constantly replace some of their less useful features with advances (better features) from other cultures.

- Great portions of Western culture come from non- Western cultures.

- Cultural features include concepts, survival techniques, information, products and technology, and even includes indigenous plants.

- No country or cultural group is dominant permanently.

- No country or cultural group dominates all fields permanently.

- Persistent differences among cultures are due to their social *histories* as well as to their social and geographic environments.

- In today's world, different cultural groups cannot remain isolated if they are to compete economically for a livelihood. They need to be able to use the knowledge of other cultures.

Answers to Discussion Questions

1. Most Americans have grown up with the U.S. leading the world in many areas such as technology, standard of living, medicine, and education. Is it important that we always lead in these areas? How can diversity in the workforce help us advance? Have we made good use of our manpower resources in the past? Why or why not?

    - History clearly shows no civilization leads forever.

    - We can learn from, and adopt ideas and practices from, other countries and cultures.

    - Workforce diversity provides more innovation than workforce homogeneity.

    - We have made poor use of our human resources in the past by excluding or limiting input from large segments of the population. We have only used part of our human resources.

2. The U.S. regularly exchanges scientists and business and industry leaders as well as technology with countries all over the world. Would the author think this is a good idea or will this just help other countries get ahead of us?

   - Sowell would probably think exchanges are a very good idea since no single culture excels in every area. He also states that "no culture has grown great in isolation..."

   - Exchanges are a benefit. Regular exchanges introduce us to advances in other cultures very rapidly which we can then quickly use.

3. In America, the management of workers by "assimilation into the workforce" is being replaced by the "integration of diversity." How would the author explain this shift in approach?

   - The author would state that integrating diversity considerations into employee management serves our purposes better than assimilating diversity because it eventually leads to higher living standards.

4. The author states that "What serves human purposes more effectively survives, while what does not, tends to decline or disappear." What aspects of American culture in general do you think may decline? What aspects of American business culture may decline?

   - "General culture" portion of question is designed to elicit opinions and general discussion of American culture. Opinions will vary as to what aspects of our culture are "valuable." Answers may concern art, music, sports, family structure, ritual, etc.

   - "Business culture" portion of question is designed to elicit discussion of management styles (e.g., command control), manufacturing dominance (e.g., computer technology, cars, etc.) and labor relations (e.g., unions).

5. List things, or the ways things are done now, that differ markedly from your parent's generation.

   - Answers will vary depending upon age range in class: the greater the age range, the greater the range of answers. Possible topics include entertainment forms and leisure pursuits, social practices, work ethic, food, diets, child rearing, education, politics, etc.

6. It has been said that English is the international language of business; Italian the international language of music; and French the international language of diplomacy. What explanation would the author give for this? Might this change?

   - The "international" languages reflect the countries which have dominated those aspects of culture.

   - On one hand, these languages can change as other nationalities become dominant. On the other hand, in some areas cultural groups/nationalities remain dominant for a long time so language change is not likely.

   - Example: In Western society the universal set of musical notation is in the Italian language and this probably won't change until some totally new form of music or instrumentation is invented.

   - Example: The U.S. could easily be overshadowed in the business world by another culture and the language of that culture could become the language of trade.

How Stereotypes Influence Opinions About Individuals

Key Points

An analogy is drawn between maps and stereotypes in which stereotypes are depicted as mental maps.

- Stereotypes, like maps, tell us about territory in the outside world.

- Mental maps (beliefs, opinions, knowledge) are learned, not innate.

- The complexity-extremity theory of stereotyping: the greater the experience with the territory, the more accurate the map (and thus, the more accurate the stereotype).

- Maps (like stereotypes) should be constructed after experiencing the territory; the territory (objects of stereotypes) should not be warped to fit the stereotype.

Answers to Discussion Questions

1. Give an example of a time in your life when your "mental map" of someone incorrectly influenced your perceptions and judgments about that person.

   - Answers often include references to first impressions of roommates, blind dates, teammates and professors who were incorrectly judged by first impressions.

2. What inaccurate perceptions may people have about you, due to your membership in some demographic group? How correct or incorrect are these perceptions?

   - Students often cite examples of being stereotyped by their demographic or ethnic groups or by physical aspects of appearance (dumb blond, lazy Hispanic, etc.,).

   - Students see others' mental maps of them as "unfair" but have more difficulty understanding that they too categorize and judge others.

3. Can you cite a specific example of a change in one of your "mental maps" since you began this course? To what do you attribute this change?

   - The more students actually experience diversity and see the effects of discrimination, the more apt they are to experience change. In descending order of impact: guest speakers, experiential exercises, films, readings and lectures seem to make the most difference.

4. How can people's "mental maps" cause problems in organizations, in personal relationships, and in international business?

Organizations:

   - Mental maps are often used as the basis of stereotypes. Candidates for jobs and promotions are prejudged and not given the same opportunities (i.e., single mothers take more time off for childcare, older workers will be sick more often etc.).

Personal Relationships:

- If our relationships are limited to people most like ourselves, we limit our opportunities to see things from new perspectives.

International Business:

- Failure to understand the needs of diverse customers

- Loss of business due to misinterpretation of others words and actions

- Incorrect assumptions that our ways of resolving conflict, motivating and rewarding employees and making decisions work in all cultures

Mental Maps

Key Points

A graphic depiction of how different ethnic and racial groups hold vastly different views of the world:

- Ethnic groups interact in mainstream social life in differing degrees.

- People's horizons, i.e., awareness of the world around them, are limited by their range of social/cultural interaction.

- Differing social classes have differing views of the world.

- Relates to Sawin article ("How Stereotypes Influence Opinions About Individuals") which depicts stereotypes as mental maps telling us about territory outside our worlds. More accurate stereotypes (more accurate mental maps) are based on more reliable knowledge gained from experience. Conversely, limited experience leads to inaccurate stereotypes (like the limited maps shown).

Answers to Discussion Questions

1. Explain why these drawings are so different from each other. To what factors do you attribute these differences?

   - These differences reflect the life experiences, and perceptions of social class experiences even more than the races of those who drew them.

   - It is interesting to note differences in specific details of these drawings such as the civic center and the Coliseum sports arena appearing only on the map drawn by the upper middle class whites from Westwood.

2. How do these groups' perceptions of their neighborhoods relate to the Sawin article on the development of stereotypes from our own "mental maps?"

   - Most students will initially attribute the differences in perception only to race, missing the advantages of social class and its relationship to the formation of our own "mental maps" and stereotypes.

Understanding Cultural Diversity

Key Points

A comparison of traditional with contemporary cultural values shows how their differences in values lead to differences in behavior which can be disadvantageous for the minority professional when not understood, but which can also become assets if balanced well.

- Not all professionals are raised with the same values.

- Minority professionals from traditional cultures are raised to value group membership and group efforts while contemporary culture values competition and individual achievement.

- The conflict with majority contemporary culture has caused traditional-culture professionals much stress when their behaviors are interpreted in terms of contemporary values or are counterproductive in a contemporary cultural setting.

- Traditional-culture professionals will have an advantage (from their group orientation) in the growing use of teams in organizations.

Answers to Discussion Questions

1. With which set of values, traditional or contemporary, were you raised?

   Many people:

   a. belong to ethnic groups, but they are groups which do not have the same traditional values as those described by Rivera or

   b. are "mixtures" and are/were not part of an ethnic cultural group. Regardless of their ages, they were raised with contemporary values.

2. There is a trend today toward the team approach in organizations. Discuss what this means in terms of the traditional and contemporary values described by the author.

   The team approach:

   a. in structure is more similar to the traditional than to the contemporary values described by the author,

   b. may be difficult to adjust to for those from contemporary backgrounds because of their background of working alone and because of the structure and diversity of membership of the team or

   c. may be easier to adjust to for those from traditional backgrounds if team members are homogeneous in outlook or, conversely, may be more difficult to adjust to if the team is heterogeneous.

3. There is also a trend in today's organizations toward more participative management styles. Discuss how this might affect someone from a traditional values background.

   - People from traditional values backgrounds are often raised to perceive great social and/or power differences between management and non-management and so they may find it very difficult to participate as equals.

4. Do you think all organizations have identical contemporary cultures? What does this mean for any worker?

- Organizational cultures, like larger cultures, are not identical even if they are generally classified as contemporary.

- Every worker has to "learn" a new culture when he/she starts a new job.

On Organizations and Diversity
Distinguishing Difference & Conflict*

Key Points

A discussion of diversity in organizations in terms of factors in the treatment of difference and ways of addressing diversity and including the positive aspects and the escalation into conflict.

Management of differences by avoidance or repression

- Avoidance Techniques: restricting associations to those with similar backgrounds; separating conflicting individuals

- Repression Techniques: refusal to allow disagreements to emerge; emphasis on team cooperation

- Appropriateness of Avoidance and Repression: useful for limiting considerations when deadlines are tight; good interim strategy to buy time to make judgments

- Dangers of Avoidance and Repression: strong resistance may develop; groupthink may result; over compatibility (stifling creativity and productivity) may occur; conflict is likely.

Differences

- Positive aspects: enriched perspectives and creativity; way to test strength of a position

- Factors affecting individuals' treatment of differences: needs, wants, goals of individual; value placed on the relationship; experiences and successes in interacting with dissimilar others

Conflicts

- Differences evoke emotions varying in intensity; intense emotions can lead to conflict.

- Transcendus exercise: students explain conflict to aliens and find themselves struggling to define it and its positive and negative values.

Answers to Discussion Questions
by Carole Parker

1. How does conflict differ from difference?

- Conflict arises when the emotions evoked in attempting to deal with differences intensify and escalate. If similarities among individuals are too weak to enable an appreciation of the difference, and the difference is heightened, the potential for conflict increases.

---

*This reading is a comparison piece intended to be read after the completion of the Transcendus exercise found in Chapter V of the text.

2. What are some dangers of avoiding and repressing differences?

- Avoiding differences can lead to "groupthink," where a group follows through with a potentially disastrous plan because different opinions are not expressed. Another consequence is overcompatibility which can lead to lower productivity.

3. Think of an experience in an organization or social setting involving avoidance or repression of difference. What were the consequences?

- For example, a friendship may have been lost because discussion of hard feelings was avoided. Also, a student may have found himself or herself in the position of assuming the most responsibility for completing a group project because of a reluctance to raise the issue with the rest of the group.

4. What are some positive uses of difference?

- More than one perspective can result in a more creative approach to problem solving. Differences are also valuable in ensuring that more aspects are considered in making decisions.

5. Can you think of any other examples of difference, other than those already mentioned in the reading?

- Organizational policies may be more equitable and fair if different interests are represented while developing the policies.

- An openness to differences may enable one to gain important information useful in revising or defending a position.

6. How can differences be managed while minimizing the risk of conflict?

- Reduce judgments and accept the legitimacy of differences. Approach managing differences with a positive attitude, a willingness to listen, and an openness to the influence of others. Encourage and promote such attitudes in the work environment.

From Affirmative Action to Affirming Diversity

Key Points

An examination of affirmative action premises and programs underscores the need to move beyond numbers recruiting into ongoing processes that better manage diversity of all types.

- Affirmative action programs as originally conceived accomplished a great deal, but are now outdated.

- Affirmative action was a transitional program to correct an imbalance, but is not adequate for developing and managing a diverse staff.

- What is needed are programs for enabling all employees to perform to their full potential where no one is advantaged or disadvantaged.

- Guidelines for organizations to manage diversity:

  1. Clarify your motivation for wanting to manage it.

  2. Clarify your vision of a diverse workforce.

  3. Expand your focus to include everyone - white males, too.

  4. Audit your corporate culture (know thyself).

  5. Modify your assumptions about how the company should operate.

  6. Modify your systems, e.g., promotion, sponsorship, performance appraisal.

  7. Modify your models of managerial and employee behavior.

  8. Help your people pioneer in trying ways to manage diversity.

  9. Apply the Special Consideration Test: Does the program give special consideration to one group or does it benefit everyone?

  10. Continue affirmative action as a platform for obtaining adiverse workforce.

Answers to Discussion Questions

1. According to Thomas, what is the primary value of Affirmative Action programs?

   - Affirmative action programs are only a mechanism for getting women and minorities into entry level positions in the organization.

2. Assess one of your current/past employers, or this college, in terms of Thomas' six step cycle. Where are these organizations in terms of managing diversity? What changes have you observed as a result of their successes or failures in this process?

- Answers vary according to the students' levels of experience, but it is helpful to list the six stages (problem recognition, intervention, great expectations, frustration, dormancy, and crisis) across the board and to check underneath where various employers are in the process.

- Be sure to make students explain how they decided to place an employer in a stage. What have they observed that makes the student think that their employer is in a particular stage? Minority and female students tend to place organizations in higher steps, particularly, numbers 3,4,5. White males tend to categorize organizations more in steps number 1 and 2.

3. Thomas writes that the "melting pot" metaphor is really a myth. Do you agree or disagree with his views? Why?

- Many students cling to the "melting pot" metaphor because they have grown up believing it is true or have heard about it so often in history classes. However, it is easy to cite examples of groups who have kept ethnic and religious customs, foods and holidays that are not "Americanized."

- Thomas makes an important point that whatever our position is on this issue outside of work, American business has kept white, male, middle class norms largely unaffected by 30 years of Affirmative Action legislation.

4. The Avon, Procter & Gamble, Digital, Corning and Xerox examples indicate that organizations can approach the challenge of managing diversity from different perspectives. Which of these seems the most directed towards improving customer service, which towards understanding its customer's needs better, and which towards promoting productivity?

- Actually an argument can be made for any of these corporation's programs improving customer service, understanding customer needs and improving productivity. The real purpose of this question is to get different students to argue for each company, so that they can come to see the connections between managing diversity and improved productivity and customer satisfaction.

5. How can an organization work towards "managing diversity" when resources are restricted due to economic downturns?

- When resources are most restricted is precisely when an organization needs to harness the energy of all of its employees, like the Atlanta example given in the reading. An organization need not launch an expensive program to have an effective one. What are its policies and procedures that are discouraging some of its people from giving 100%? How can it use internal resources like employee groups, to improve its understanding of diversity issues?

6. What are some of the advantages for white males in a company that has managing diversity as a strategic imperative?

- If the program is well done, it is inclusive of white male issues, too. Managing diversity is about change and understanding, not about "us" and "them." Many white males are searching to understand others and welcome an opportunity to learn. If this group is automatically stereotyped as being outside of the loop of diversity issues, the program will not work.

Managing Cultural Diversity: *Implications for Organizational Competitiveness*

Key Points

The "arguments and research data on how managing diversity can create a competitive advantage are reviewed." (Cox & Blake)

- With increasing ethnic and gender diversity and business becoming more globalized, managers must now be concerned with cultural differences.

- The literature says that diversity is valuable to an organization without citing wupporting research. This article reviews the research.

- with well-managed diversity, research suggests that:

   Costs are lower due to higher productivity, lower absenteeism and lower employee turnover

   Resource-Acquisition is better, i.e., companies with the best reputations of employee treatment get their pick of the best talent.

   Marketing is better. Both in overseas and domestic markets, ethnic employees understand ethnic consumers better than outsiders do.

   Creativity is greater. Heterogeneity in work teams leads to more perspectives and greater innovation and creativity in planning

   Problem-solving is better. A richer and wider variety of experiences is brought to bear on problems. Less "groupthink" occurs.

   Note. The quality of decision-making is best when there is neither too much diversity nor too much homogeneity.

   System Flexibility is greater. Research has shown women, racio-ethnic minorities and bilinguals to have "especially flexible cognitive structures." Additionally, managing cultural diversity results in less static and standardized policies and greater organizational adaptability.

- Transformation of a traditional organization into a truly multicultural one requires top management commitment, training in awareness and skill building, research on diversity-related issues, culture and management systems audits and follow-up (monitoring) of the changes.

Answers to Discussion Questions

1. This article discusses the benefits of worker diversity in terms of gender and race/ethnicity. Do you think the same benefits can occur with diversity of physical disability? age? Sexual orientation? Explain why or why not.

Physical Disability:	yes
Age:	yes
Sexual Orientation:	yes

Explanations center on the six competitive advantages outlined in the article: cost, resource acquisition, marketing creativity, problem solving and organizational flexibility as well as social responsibility.

2. Why is excessive heterogeneity (diversity) not recommended in this article? How do you avoid this?

- The author feels that excessive diversity impedes group cohesion and cohesion is related to the success of the group. There needs to be a core of similarity - common values, norms and goals to aid people in working together.

3. List some of the possible reasons that women and minorities are often less satisfied with their jobs than are white men.

Primary Reasons:

- Frustration over career growth, i.e., lack of opportunity and slow rate of progress

- Cultural conflict with white male cultural norms

- Difficulties of balancing multiple roles

- Lower salaries

4. How does an organizations's failure to manage women and minorities effectively translate into unnecessary costs? How can more effective management of these groups lead to competitive advantages?

- Unnecessary Costs: The turnover and absentee rates are higher for unhappy employees and are expensive for an organization.

- Dissatisfied workers are not as productive as those who are satisfied.

- Competitive Advantages: Companies known for treating women and minorities well will have their pick of the most talented of these groups when recruiting.

- Diversity of people means greater diversity of perspectives, i.e., greater creativity in terms of problem solving and meeting the needs of diverse customer markets.

- Better decisions result due to greater heterogeneity of approaches.

- Well-managed diversity can lead to greater flexibility in the system - greater sensitivity in responding to changes in the business environment.

5. If some managers do not seem to be handling the diversity of their personnel well, how might the performance appraisal and reward process be used to encourage them to improve?

- Performance appraisal, bonuses and raises can rest in part on how well the manager is handling diversity, i.e., the recruiting, developing and promoting of members of diverse groups.

Moving Forward on Reverse Discrimination

Key Points

Arguments for and against affirmative actions programs are presented leading to the conclusion that these preferential treatment policies do not violate the principle of equal justice for all and therefore should be continued.

Opponent's Arguments:

1. Affirmative action violates the principle of distributive justice because it leads to reverse discrimination. Preferential treatment treats one group of citizens differently.

2. Affirmative action violates the principle of compensatory justice which requires compensation for loss only from those who harmed or deprived the victim, not from those who did no harm.

3. The merit system should apply.

Rebuttal to Distributive Justice Argument:

The basis for preferential treatment is not race (i.e., a class or group characteristic), but a history of discrimination and victimization. Such a history is due to:

• Housing patterns which have placed economically disadvantaged (largely minorities) in poor inner city areas.

• School patterns, an outgrowth of housing patterns, which concentrate large numbers of poor minorities in crowded, poor quality schools.

• Housing and school patterns which have meant that top level managers and minorities are often uncomfortable with each other due to limited interaction as they grew up.

• Blacks are not equal to whites in ability to compete for the reasons given above, so the situation is one of unequals being treated unequally (by affirmative action) which does not violate the distributive justice principle.

Rebuttal to Compensatory Justice Argument:

• The only thing whites lose is maintaining the job-competing advantages that their history of social advantages has given them. Rebuttal to Merit Argument:

• Basing employment decisions on the merit system implies that a merit system exists, but it really doesn't. Many employment decisions are based on "who you know" and blacks are rarely part of the mentor, network or old boy systems.

• Another weakness of merit arguments is that it may be more important to compensate for past injustice than to consider merit.

• Merit in management is very difficult to measure. Race can be an element of merit, e.g., having black representation in social institutions, black police for inner-city neighborhoods, etc. can be a benefit to all.

Answers to Discussion Questions

1. In this article the authors argue the merits of Affirmative Action from several viewpoints. Which of their arguments makes the most sense to you and which the least? Why?

   - Answers will differ by individual. Some will think that Affirmative Action is the right thing to do from an ethical perspective, while others will argue that like it or not, it is the law. Others will see no merits in AA programs and cite examples of people that they feel got their jobs because they were members of protected classes.

2. How can managers and organizations overcome the negative backlash associated with quotas?

   - Any manager can hire or promote a minority or a woman but it may take more effort or slightly different recruiting methods to hire a qualified person. Backlash most often occurs when unqualified people are hired to fill a "quota" system. Organizations need to be held accountable by linking hiring, development and promotional goals of qualified minorities to management reward/appraisal systems.

3. If you are Caucasian, assume for a moment that you are a member of a racial minority group. What problems might you now experience when applying for a job for which you are qualified, that as a white person you have not experienced?

   - or -

If you are a racial minority, assume for a moment that you are Caucasian. How would you anticipate that applying for a job, for which you are qualified, would be different from what you have experienced in your own job searches?

   - The purpose of this question is to help each group to understand the circumstances experienced by the other group. Minorities often perceive that white people have an advantage in applying for a job (i.e., most interviewers are white, most companies have predominantly white employees, etc.). In contrast, white people often feel that minorities can get hired even if they are less than qualified due to AA/EEO.

4. As a class, discuss why the answers to question #3 were different for the two groups.

   - This question is designed to lead to a discussion of differences in perception due to socialization, life experiences, stereotypes and lack of open communication.

5. By demographics we know that the workforce is becoming increasingly non-white. Assume for a moment that the government has eliminated all equal employment and affirmative action programs. In the next ten years would non-whites and women be represented in proportion to their numbers in the workforce and/or in higher management? Why or why not?

   - Some students will offer the argument that it is evolutionary, i.e., only a matter of time, before women and minorities reach upper level jobs in organizations because they can get entry level jobs under Equal Opportunity protection.

   - Others may point out that 30 years of EEO/AA have led to women only holding three percent, and racial minorities one percent, of the Fortune 500 hundred top corporate jobs.

   - Even with these current laws and programs, these groups are not represented in proportionate numbers after 30 years. Consequently, there is little to suggest that this would be an evolutionary process, especially if legal protection were removed.

Many Minorities Feel Torn by Experience of Affirmative Action

Key Points

An illustration with specific examples shows that affirmative action has drawbacks as well as advantages for minorities. It points out that:

- Not all minorities favor affirmative action, including those who have benefitted from it.

- Affirmative action has opened the doors of employment to jobs previously closed to minorities.

- Affirmative action recipients of jobs and promotions are often assumed to be less qualified than their peers.

- Some employees hire poorly qualified minorities just to fill affirmative action quotas thus fostering the belief that all minorities benefitting from affirmative action are poorly qualified.

Answers to Discussion Questions

1. If you were a manager in the Birmingham, Alabama Fire Department, what would you do to improve racial harmony?

   Some steps: (students are encouraged to add others):

   - Use wider and better recruiting to get better qualified minorities.

   - Offer better education and training for minorities.

   - Offer education programs for supervisors in handling diversity.

   - Offer mentoring programs.

2. What kinds of things might organizations of all kinds (business, political, academic) do if they find they are filling their affirmative action quotas with poorly qualified minorities?

   Some things:

   - Use wider and better recruiting.

   - Offer education and training programs for all candidates.

   - Offer mentoring programs.

   - Train managers on the differences between EEO/AA and managing diversity.

   - Include hiring and developing and promoting qualified minorities as part of managers' performance review goals.

3. How far should affirmative action go, i.e., at what point should it stop? Should it be abolished? Should there be hiring quotas? Promotion advantages for minorities?

- This opinion question is designed to get students to seriously consider all facets of the arguments for and against affirmative action provisions presented in the reading.

4. From the perspective of organizations, what are the benefits of affirmative action? In what ways is it a detriment?

Among the benefits:

- It opens doors to employment in organizations which have traditionally been closed to minority group members.

- It forces managers to rethink their traditional recruiting and selection practices.

- It fosters a wider range of perspectives and solutions to organizational problems.

- It allows minorities an opportunity to rise in organizations.

- It can improve race and gender relations.

Among the detriments:

- Resentment and backlash from the majority can result.

- More poorly qualified candidates can get hired.

- More poorly qualified candidates can get promoted.

- It can worsen race relations.

- It fosters tokenism when managers settle for any minority candidate who can fill a quota category.

Equal Employment Responsibilities of Multinational Corporations

Key Points

The historic development of legal applications of equal employment opportunity laws to U.S. firms operating in other countries is traced with an examination of the economic, legal, ethical and discretionary responsibilities of such firms.

- Historically, equal opportunity laws have not automatically been applied to overseas employees of U.S. firms; courts have ruled against it, Congress has mandated for it.

- Currently, U.S. companies are bound by host country laws. If no laws exist, equal opportunity laws apply.

- Economic disadvantages occur to the U.S. company when host country culture (and prejudice) and practices conflict with employee rights.

- Economic advantages occur in the more effective use of human resources and building of employee morale.

- Legal disadvantages include greater likelihood of corporations being sued by overseas employees.

- Legal advantages include the setting of standards often adopted by corporate counterparts in other cultures.

- Ethical disadvantages stem from the fact that home country practices and standards do not have legal standing in the host country.

- Ethical advantages stem from expectations that home country ethical standards will apply and the U.S. standard of non-biased workplace activity is reaffirmed.

- Discretionary considerations are those practices and policies which go beyond the legal require-ments, e.g., special benefits, sensitivity training, support groups, etc. which may influence host countries toward equitable worker treatment.

Answers to Discussion Questions

1. Suppose a U.S. company has an overseas facility located in a country where the cultural norms dictate that it is socially unacceptable to put women or certain other nationalities in supervisory positions. Should the company honor local customs in this regard?

Business Perspective. If the company does put these groups in managerial positions, the extent of "potential dam-age" will depend on how socially unacceptable the practice is to the local culture, whether the managers are super-vising locals or U.S. nationals, or both, and how powerful (important to the local economy) the company is. The company must also weigh the waste of human resources, lowered employee morale, loyalty and economic efficiency costs of not putting these people into management positions.

Moral and Social Perspective. The authors state that "As members of the global community, multi-national compa-nies have a moral interest in the observance of those rules [employee rights]."

2. Suppose the company in question 1 chooses to hire or promote women or "low status" minorities into supervisory positions. What business advantages might result? What business disadvantages might result?

Advantages: Better quality employees
               Better employee morale and loyalty
               Better productivity Better marketing

Disadvantages: Refusal of local staff to cooperate with minority supervisors
               Boycotting by local consumers
               Difficulties with local officials

3. Our laws clearly indicate that the U.S. believes in fair treatment and opportunity for all employees. Many countries; for historic, ethnocentric and/or economic reasons, do not share these beliefs.

If the host country has no regulations, do you think our companies located there should "influence" the host country to accept our beliefs?

If the host country does have discriminatory laws, should our companies "lobby" for change toward our beliefs?

- Discussion and opinion should center on what forms "influence" and lobbying" might take: e.g., by setting an example with company policy and practices of fair treatment and employee opportunity; by interfering in host country politics to support the enactment of legislation, etc. Students find some practices acceptable and others not acceptable.

4. There are many U.S. organizations overseas which are non-profit. Some are charitable and depend for success upon acceptance by, and close relations with, the local people. Should these organizations be required to follow U.S. employment laws if the host country has strong prejudices against employing or promoting certain groups? Why or why not?

Opinion question designed to provide thought and discussion on ethical organizational issues.

Xerox Makes It Work

Key Points

- Organizations may have successes and failures while learning to manage diverse employees.

- Xerox acknowledged "white backlash" issues and addressed the needs of white males in their diversity programs.

- Minority caucus groups play a key role in the retention and promotion of diverse employees by providing informal networking and mentoring support.

- Xerox has moved beyond an AA/EEO legal requirements approach more towards the type of organization envisioned by R. Roosevelt Thomas in his article, From Affirmative Action to Affirming Diversity.

Answers to Discussion Questions

1. Make a list of the reasons, in addition to AA/EEO compliance, that could motivate a company like Xerox to take a pro-active stance on diversity.

   - Being located or doing a lot of business in communities that have a high percentage of minority residents (Note: Rochester NY, where Xerox is headquartered has a high percentage of black residents and was the scene of race riots in 1964 and 1967).

   - The personal values of the CEO, board of directors or of top management

   - A realization that once a company has established a good track record for hiring, developing and promoting women and minorities, it is far easier to recruit the most talented ones

   - A sense of social responsibility in terms of doing the right thing for society

   - Conducting business in a multi-national environment

   - Having a customer base that can be best understood and served by women and minorities

2. Evaluate your list in terms of some of the key factors currently associated with management today: total quality, productivity, globalization, etc.

Total quality

   - Requires the best workers regardless of their race or gender

   - Drawing from a wider pool of diverse employees, a company has a better opportunity to tap into more creative and innovative ways of solving problems and doing business

Productivity

   - If diverse employees feel included and satisfied with the way that the organization treats them, they are less apt to leave, be absent etc., and more apt to work up to their full potential

- Doing business in different countries can be enhanced when a company's employees speak the language and understand the culture.

3. Prepare an argument that supports Rand's statement, "Blacks do not have the luxury of being mediocre."

- If one minority group member does not perform, there is a tendency to generalize his/her behavior to other minority group members which makes it more difficult for them to be hired, promoted, etc., in the future

- Minorities are more visible and their mistakes are more apt to be apparent to members of the majority culture

- Some people are just waiting to point out the mistakes of a minority employee

4. The Xerox article illustrates that managing diversity can include white males in addition to minority workers. Why is it also important to address this often overlooked aspect of diversity ?

- Backlash from white males may be counter productive and lead to a lack of commitment and motivation from a high proportion of the workforce

- White males still hold over 95% of the top corporate jobs and their support is needed to obtain the programs and resources that promote diversity

- White males are in the ideal position to hire, develop, promote and mentor minorities

Additional References

Lesley, Elizabeth. "Sticking it out at Xerox by sticking together." Business Week, November 2, 1993, p. 77.

Sessa, Valerie I. (1992). Managing Diversity at the Xerox Corporation: Balanced Workforce Goals and Caucus Groups, from Susan E. Jackson & Associates Diversity in the Workplace: Human Resources Initiative, New York: The Guilford Press. pp. 37-64.

On the Dimensions of Diversity

The Job Makes the Person

Key Points

An analysis is made of how opportunity, power and tokenism explains common perceptions and stereotypes (as well as the behaviors) of women in organizations.

Opportunity:

- Low Ambition. Women are less ambitious than men, but most women are in low-level, dead-end jobs with blocked opportunity. Women in high-ranking jobs don't appear to be less ambitious than males.

- Men in low level jobs also have low ambition while those in high ranking jobs have higher ambition.

Power:

- Most people don't want female bosses because "they are too picky."

- Few females, regardless of position or title, have real power.

- Male and female managers without power (often coupled with being unsure of oneself) frequently become "punitive, petty tyrants," emphasizing rules and repressing innovation and creavity.

Tokenism:

- Women at the top are often tokens. They stand out and are treated differently from the men. The same situation holds for blacks. Tokens are: isolated from the group and its information network; the subject of hostile, raunchy talk; expected to play a stereotyped role; must work twice as hard as male counterparts; and are constantly under the pressure of display in a fishbowl.

- To change this oppressive cycle, the organizational structure which blocks opportunity and power and which creates token situations must be changed.

Answers to Discussion Questions

1. What would you do if you were a manager and you wanted your people to be more task-oriented?

- Openly discuss and plan opportunities for advancement based on performance levels. Dead-end jobs reduce motivation, lead workers to spend more time on developing peer groups to obtain social satisfaction on the job and foster resentment toward the management and toward new employees brought in for higher level jobs.

- Link high performance levels with increased opportunities for additional training, development and education.

- Understand that from a worker's viewpoint, the amount of work accomplished may be quite different than from a manager's perspective.

- Realize that everyone is not motivated by the same things. For example, some people may be afraid that being singled out as a star performer by the organization will isolate them from their co-workers.

45

2. In view of the Kanter findings, what advice would you give to anyone entering (or already in) an employment situation in which they are a minority?

- Find a mentor.

- Try to develop a support network either on the job or through professional organizations.

- Try to depersonalize any incidents of minor "tokenism" which may occur because some people see you as representing a whole group (women, Hispanics, etc.) rather than as an individual.

- Work at developing more self-confidence in terms of being yourself; not hiding your abilities and accomplishments and working to avoid acting in stereotypical roles that you may feel are expected of you (such as women always taking the notes at a meeting, etc.).

- Assess your own behavior for clues that you may be responsible for your lack of progress (i.e., not contributing your ideas in meetings, not being willing to take on challenging assignments, and not being willing to do extra work).

3. Employees who are critical and resentful are often frustrated and blocked people who are not very productive and who act as depressors on others. What might be done to improve their morale and productivity?

- Empower managers. They need to feel comfortable, empowered and sure of themselves. When they don't, they are likely to focus on minute details instead of the big picture.

- Have an honest discussion about their career goals. Explain how their present behavior may be blocking their opportunities for advancement.

- Try to discover what motivates them. It may be quite different from what motivates the manager. Do not assume that they are motivated by opportunities for advancement or raises. For example, they may have personal reasons for preferring a more flexible schedule to care for an aged parent or a child.

- Provide training and development opportunities.

- Consider a lateral move to a job that may be more personally satisfying to them.

4. Talent, innovation and creativity are immensely important to organizations today. How do you develop managers who will reward these qualities? Under what circumstances do managers suppress or fail to reward these qualities?

- Provide organizational rewards and support for creative, innovative work. Do not reward "business as usual" with promotions and raises.

- Create a safe culture where it is all right to make an occasional mistake.

- Managers actively suppress or fail to reward creativity and innovation when they are threatened and feel powerless as in question number three.

5. Often in organizations, minorities do not exhibit much ambition and seem to "stick together." Apply Kanter's observations about women to such minorities. Relate this to Rivera's discussion of Hispanic traditional values.

- Since people are often most comfortable communicating and being with people like themselves who share common interests and values, they tend to band together to create a more comfortable atmosphere. Couple this with being in what is often considered as a dead-end job and it is understandable why women may create peer groups on the job for meeting their social needs and for mutual support and enjoyment.

- In Rivera's article, Hispanic traditional values are described as group oriented rather than as individualistic. Members of such cultures are likely to exhibit the same behaviors as the women described above when they are part of an organizational culture that is different from the one in which they are most comfortable.

Why Women Aren't Making It to the Top

Key Points

A series of cases of women in the senior ranks of organizations and their problems gaining power are presented.

- Men are ambivalent about women having and using power and often keep women out of senior ranks because they think women can't exercise power.

- Women admit they don't always go after power as aggressively as men or as they should.

- A confused male image of women causes problems: Top executives defer to the CEO and when women defer, it is seen as a sign of weakness and calls up images of wives and mothers.

- Technical skill is required at lower and middle ranks and men can accept women with such skill, but other skills are usually more important at top levels where power handling is important.

- Women usually have to fight for power at the top; men often withhold it by a variety of techniques illustrated in the cases.

Answers to Discussion Questions

1. None of the women in this article cited other women as mentors or role models. How do you account for this?

- There may be few women in a powerful enough position to be of help to them.

- They may have had mentors in the past at lower levels of the organization but not at this level.

- They may have wanted to think that they did not need the help of mentors.

2. Make a list of the possible factors that may account for the "glass ceiling" that keeps women from top corporate jobs. Then divide the list into the factors that women can and can't control. Is there any disagreement between the men and women in the class about which factors women can't control? How do you account for these differences in perception? Sample list:

CAN CONTROL	CAN NOT CONTROL
Willingness to take risks	Prejudice and stereotypes
Willingness to work hard, and get more education	Double standards for maleand female performance & behavior
Seeking out a mentor management	Highly conservative practices
Making their career aspirations known to superiors	
Willingness to take challenging assignments that increase visibility	

49

- Women tend to make a longer list of the things that they can not control and men tend to make a longer list of the things that women can control. Different perspectives on the problem lead to different answers.

3. How can a woman be her own worst enemy in terms of career advancement? Cite specific examples from the cases, articles, or your own work experiences.

- Women who are clearly out for themselves

- Women who feel that they deserve special treatment because of their gender

- Women who use the fact that they are women to take special advantage of situations

- Women who are unwilling to work hard, take career risks, get more education, etc. but who complain that they are not promoted because of their gender

- Students may generalize from single experiences. For example, having had one picky female boss, a woman who does not speak out in meetings, etc. Many of their examples may relate more to a lack of power and different communication styles than to poor management.

4. Assess Prenderville's boss's method of presenting her candidacy to the board. Was it fair, clever, realistic, deceitful, etc? Explain your answer.

- It was fair because gender was not an issue; clever in terms of how he approached the board; and realistic in terms of her qualifications. (One of the authors had a very similar experience herself!) This experience is often described as deceitful by young males; more positively by females and older males.

5. In terms of effective management, contrast Prenderville's boss's method of approaching the board with Peg Simpson's boss's failure to appoint her to the board.

- Prenderville's boss presented an objective case based on qualifications while Simpson's boss exhibited more covert actions and less mentoring, and more reliance on the "old boy network."

Do Women Make Better Managers?

Key Points

The controversy surrounding differences in male and female management styles is discussed.

Controversies:

Do males tend to have hierarchical, authoritarian styles and females more consensus-building, participatory styles? Judy Rosener's paper started this debate.

In this era of corporate downsizing and restructuring, which management style is best? Some say: authoritarian, because effective leaders must make hard decisions. Others say consensus-building is better because employee motivation is crucial.

Agreement:

Old definition of management must be expanded to fit the globalization of the marketplace.

Answers to Discussion Questions

1. Do you agree or disagree that women make better managers for today's organizations? Cite specific examples from your work experience to back up your answer.

   - A case can be made for either position. On one side, women tend to favor more communication, employee participation, and use less hierarchial models which work well in more team-centered, decentralized organizations. However, in a time of rapid organizational change and restructuring, the more masculine take-charge-and-lead model may also offer some advantages.

2. Explain the major differences between "transformational" and "transactional" leaders. Which of these styles are you most comfortable working under? Why? Which of these styles would you feel most comfortable using as a manager? Why? Do you think that your answers to these questions were influenced by your gender? Why or why not?

TRANSFORMATIONAL	TRANSACTIONAL
Includes a high degree of worker input and participation	Based on rewards for good performance and punishments for poor performance
Seeks consensus	More authoritarian
Decentralized	Hierarchial

   - Few students will admit that their answers were influenced by their gender, but women tend to favor the transformational, and men the transactional, models.

3. How do people develop different management "styles?"

- Styles, like personalities, are a product of our socialization, work and personal experiences and culture. Role models, both positive and negative, organizational culture, norms and values may also influence our ways of managing.

4. What can female managers learn from men and what can male managers learn from women?

- Women can learn that there are times when due to time constraints, worker inexperience or incompetence, emergencies, or organizational culture, they may need to be more authoritarian. Sometimes the person in charge simply has to make the decisions.

- Men can learn to encourage participation, to welcome input from their subordinates and to be more sensitive to the people and process issues of the organization.

5. What factors in an organization's culture could account for one style working better than the other in that particular organization?

- The design of the work, whether it requires repetition or autonomy; how the personal needs of the employees are met – on or off the job; the gender and ethnic composition of the workforce; the norms and values of the organization particularly in its attitudes towards risk, reward, control, trust, degree of decentralization.

White Privilege and Male Privilege:
A Personal Account of Coming to See Correspondences through Work in Women's Studies

Key Points

The reluctance of males and whites to recognize that they have special unearned privileges which give them advantages is examined the article concludes with an extensive list of everyday, taken-for-granted, white privileges.

- Males and whites are taught not to recognize their privileges; they can admit that others are underprivileged, but can't see the corollary to this.

- Denial of male over-privilege is seen in a variety of arguments males make against changing the academic curriculum to reduce male centrality and dominance.

- Author lists 46 special privileges she (and other whites) take for granted daily – privileges not enjoyed by nonwhites.

Answers to Discussion Questions

1. What does the author mean by the concept of "white privilege?"

   - Being unaware of the unearned advantages of being white

2. Re-read the author's list of 46 examples of white privilege. Select the five examples that seem the most signifi cant in helping you to understand that white people are privileged. Explain your selections.

   - Answers vary here but some examples are usually more difficult for white students to comprehend (e.g., example numbers 2, 5, 8, 20, 24, 35) than others which they seem to understand (as in numbers 3, 12, 46). This article can add to a productive class dialogue, particularly there are minorities present in the class who will share their reactions to these 46 items. Many white students think that legislation has "taken care of" some of these examples of racial privilege. Minorities know that this is far from the reality.

3. In addition to white privilege, the author also cites examples of heterosexual privilege. Develop a list of privileges that the able-bodied enjoy that the physically challenged do not experience.

   - Answers should come from the class. Small groups can be used to develop ideas. Sometimes you will have to give one or two examples to get the class moving (i.e., I can choose any seat on a bus or an airline. I can use any rest room. I am not dependent on anyone to dress me in the morning).

4. Most of us have experienced privilege in some form. Describe an example from your experience.

   - Many students have difficulty with this question. An example for Christians is the emphasis put on the celebration of Christmas as though it is everyone's holiday.

   - If the class is composed of students of traditional age, bring to their attention some "privileges" from the past such as the "help wanted male" job ads, lower life and car insurance rates for females, the fact that in many states men were not allowed by law to teach below the 6th grade, etc. Students can also be assigned to ask their parents and grandparents for additional examples.

5. How does this article help you to understand the oppression that members of other groups may experience?

- The author's unique approach offers an opportunity to understand that we may be unaware of how many unearned "privileges " we have by virtue of our race or sexual preference. This can lead to an interesting dialogue about how 30 years of EEO/AA legislation have not, and may never, totally level the playing field for everybody.

Aspirations and Apprehension:
Employees with Disabilities

Key Points

The current status of employment of the disabled is depicted using biographic sketches of disabled employees, employment statistics, and an analysis of the changing employability picture.

- Traditionally, media have fostered unflattering stereotypes of persons with disabilities.

- Changes affecting employment:

- Mainstreaming and rights-focused schooling are helping employability.

- Job accommodations are becoming expected of employers.

- A.D.A. legislation assures access and accommodations for persons with disabilities to employment, public buildings, public transportation, and telecommunications.

- Employers have increasing technical aids and support services to help in providing accommodations.

Answers to Discussion Questions
by Bonnie Prince

Assume you are an employer with a position opening for which William may be suitable. Consider the following questions. Also examine the issues in the context of other kinds of disabilities. For example, ask the same questions for persons who have sensory, mobility or communication limitations; for persons with a guide dog, care attendant or assistive technology device such as a talking computer; for persons who do not appear to be disabled, but announce they have a mental health or learning disability or a chronic illness; and for persons who specify a kind of accommodation they will need for the job.

(To the instructor: The following points are meant for discussion. They are not intended as a definitive legal interpretation of disability issues or the Americans with Disabilities Act. For more thorough analysis, instructors are referred to resources cited in the article.)

1. What are the misunderstandings or biases that employers might have about hiring a person like William? What are some legitimate concerns? What are positive reasons or advantages for hiring persons with disabilities?

> Consider that the outward manifestation of a disability (e.g., wheelchair, uncontrolled physical movements, slurred speech, difficulty with eye contact) often detract from or mask adequate or superior work skills or intellectual ability.

> Employers may legitimately consider the safety of others if a "direct threat" is present (specific risk of substantial harm for which accommodation is not possible), or "undue hardship" to the business will occur (excessive cost or a fundamental change in the nature of business). However, employers must guard against assuming that their stereotypes, myths and general speculations about disabling conditions can be applied automatically to the specific applicant, and that perceived hardships, in reality, cannot be handled successfully by their business.

Advantages can be the same as when hiring any person. For example, hiring a person with a disability may bring superior training, new skills or access to new resources or contacts into the company, just as hiring any person would. Employers who hire a person with a disability are complying with the law and participating in the national trend toward increasing diversity in the work place. However,they should not expect any special recognition or pat on the back, since most persons with disabilities prefer to be treated like any other employee.

2. What should William (or anyone with a disability) put on a resume when seeking a position from an employer who does not know about his condition? How should such a person refer to the disability during the interview, if at all?

> Advice appears to be split. Unlike other minority groups, there is no affirmative action requirement for persons with disabilities; thus disclosure is not necessarily advantageous. Persons who reveal their disability in advance may, however, alert the employer to potential discrimination issues, thus clearing the way for focusing on the job itself.

> On the other hand, not revealing one's disability allows the person to sell his or her skills, talents and credentials, and not appear to be featuring or "using" the disability.

> However, if an accommodation will be needed during the interview or during the job itself, the person with the disability will have to openly request this at some point. The timing of this request should be considered in relation to the applicant's goal of managing the first impressions of the employer. The applicant's primary purpose should be to market his or her talents in relation to the job as the employer envisions it, and to be hired for the job based on abilities.

3. If you know in advance that a person like William will require special access for the interview, what sort of preparations, if any, should you make? If a person with a disabling condition appears for an interview without your advanced knowledge, what should you do?

> Persons with disabilities who are seeking a job are generally self-sufficient about their own needs and will make known any accommodation requests without being asked.

> Special concern expressed by employers (even when well intentioned) is usually unnecessary, and could be interpreted as an illegal inquiry about the disability itself.

> With care, an employer who foresees a special need may offer an accommodation, such as extra time, assistance with application forms, an elevator key, a reserved parking space, relocation of the interview or similar courtesy.

> In a specific accommodation is requested by the applicant, the employer is legally required to provide that accommodation or offer a similar, equivalent system of support.

4. What questions are appropriate for the employer to ask during the interview? What questions are inappropriate or illegal? Are special interviewing techniques called for? What are some mistakes interviewer might make? How do job descriptions fit into the picture?

While the following lists are not exhaustive, they represent several pre-employment issues:

Appropriate:

> Any question that is relevant to performing all job-related functions of the work to be done which also is asked of all other applicants. (Examples: Can you arrive at work at 8:30 a.m.? Can you drive a delivery vehicle? Can you work 40 hours a week? Can you operate a cash register?)

A request to demonstrate a job-related function of the work to be done which is also requested of all other applicants. (For example: Please demonstrate how you operate this cash register.)

Inappropriate or illegal questions, common mistakes:

Any question about an applicant's physical or mental condition, about whether a disability exists, about the nature or severity of a known or presumed disability, or about the effects of a disability. (Examples: Do you have any health problems? Have you ever required hospitalization? Have you ever needed counseling? Are you seeing a psychiatrist now? How often are you absent from work? Are you taking medication for any condition? How you ever received disability benefits? Will you require time off for your medical appointments? Does you arm present problems for you?)

Requesting a medical examination or performance test of an applicant with a disability which is not requested of all other applicants.

Asking the applicant's former employer about an actual or perceived disability of an applicant. (However, job references not related to a disability may be requested.)

Special interviewing techniques:

Special interviewing techniques, unless an accommodation has been specifically requested by the applicant, are in danger of being considered discriminatory and should be avoided by employers.

While not a "technique," an approach employers should take is to maintain an open mind and not form conclusions based on their impressions or assumptions about the disability. They should look for the person's abilities and evaluate how these can be an asset to the company. They should also remain open to a variety of possibilities for accommodations.

Job descriptions:

Rewriting job descriptions to identify the "essential functions" of the job before opening the position will help employers evaluate all applicants fairly. A function is "essential" if it is among the specific job's key elements (not secondary or marginal in this particular job, or applicable to a general group of jobs, but not necessarily this one). Other criteria for essentialness are that only a limited number of other employees in the company could perform the function, or the function is so specialized that it is the key reason for hiring an employee.

Any standard of performance, qualification, special testing procedures, or credential required for the position should be set in advance and stated in the job description. Such standards must be related directly to the job and must not be phrased to exclude persons with disabilities, with or without accommodations.

5. What issues can be applied to the final decision about whether or not to hire William? What issues are not legitimate? What are some "gray areas?" How does the Americans with Disabilities Act apply?

As in the interview, hiring must be based on the qualifications and abilities of the applicant in relation to the"essential functions" of the job. Provision of accommodations to support job performance must also be a consideration.

William's levels of experience, credentials, knowledge and skills (after any required accommodations are included) may be compared to those of other candidates, similar to the hiring decision for any applicant.

Gray areas include imprecise definitions for "essential" job functions, "reasonable" accommodations, and "undue" hardship in the A.D.A. Employers should obtain knowledgeable legal counsel if they have questions.

The A.D.A. broadens these issues to all employers, not just those who receive federal funds or who are public employers.

6. What approach should managers take to providing job accommodations? What kinds of accommodations are suitable for William? Or for other kinds of disabilities? Where can a manager get technical information or assistance about accommodations?

An employer must make a "reasonable accommodation" to assure an applicant with a disability is not discriminated against. Accommodations vary widely. They may include actions such as job restructuring, modifying a work schedule, rebuilding a work location for physical access, obtaining a technical device or piece of equipment, assigning another employee to assist with or take over some job functions, developing a flexible leave policy, or allowing a care attendant to accompany the employee.

The expense for an accommodation usually must be covered the employer. Unless "undue hardship" can be demonstrated, the expanse cannot be the excuse for not hiring an applicant with a disability.

Cooperative initiatives and assistance can often be developed with local offices of state vocational rehabilitation ("VR") agencies. Other resources at the end of the article offer additional support.

7. How should a manager cope with a disability acquired by an existing employee?

The issues are similar to hiring new employees, with the additional consideration that transfer or redesign of a job may be implemented for a disabled or returning employee.

Employers cannot reduce the nature of their company's benefits for a specific employee who becomes disabled.

8. For persons with disabilities, how should a manager handle organizational systems of feedback and coaching, performance evaluation, job descriptions, promotion or dismissal?

In addition to hiring, all attributes of regular jobs must be applied in a nondiscriminatory manner to persons with disabilities, including benefits, professional development, opportunities for advancement, recreational opportunities, etc. Similarly, nondiscrimination must be incorporated into any change or reduction of job benefits, meaning these must affect all workers.

Maintaining an open communication system with an employee who has a disability is important. Problems, misunderstandings or even legal action related to the disability can usually be avoided.

Employers should review their biases about the capability of an employee with a disability of performing more sophisticated or managerial roles within the company.

One should not assume that such persons are merely grateful to have any job, or content to remain in their current position forever. Their skills and experience with the company, possibly with additional training, advanced electronic equipment or flexible job design, should be given equal consideration by an employer who is implementing human resource development strategies for the company.

Offering an accommodation to an employee with a disability who is performing poorly should preclude any disciplinary action.

As with all problematic supervisory situations, careful documentation of any issues or disciplinary actions is always wise.

References and Resources

<u>Ability</u>. A colorful, up-scale magazine with relevant articles about celebrities, modern living, employment opportunities and technology trends for persons with disabilities. P. P. Box 4140, Irvine CA, 92716-9919.

Ackerstein, J. (1994). <u>The Americans with Disability Act: What supervisors need to know</u>. The Business Skills Express Series. New York, NY: Business One Irwin/Mirror Press.

American Foundation for the Blind (1986). <u>The future of work for disabled people: Employment and the new technology</u>. New York, NY.

Bowe, F. (1990). <u>Employment and people with disabilities: Challenges for the nineties</u>. OSERS News in Print, Vol. III, No. 3. Washington, DC: U.S. Department of Education: Winter, 1990.

Casper, M. W. (1993). <u>Seasons of Change—The Americans with Disabilities Act: Implementation in the Work Place</u>. Journal of Rehabilitation, Vol. 17, No. 3.

Internet. Resources are available on Internet. For example, use the Gopher at "dewey.lib.ncsu.edu."

Job Accommodation Network (JAN). Toll-free Number: 1-800-JAN-PCEH or, in West Virginia, 1-800-JAN-INWV, by both voice or TDD, 8:00 a.m. to 8:00 p.m.

Kiernan, W. E., Schalock, R. L. & Knutson, K. (1989). Economic and demographic trends influencing employment opportunities for adults with disabilities. In W. E. Kiernan & R. L. Schalock, <u>Economics, industry, and disability: A look ahead</u>. Baltimore: Paul H. Brookes, 1989.

Kraus, L. E. & Stoddard, S. (1991). <u>Chartbook on work disability in the United States</u>. An InfoUse Report. Washington, D.C.: National Institution on Disability and Rehabilitation Research.

<u>Mouth: The Voice of Disability Rights</u>. An ironic, humorous, sometimes irreverent magazine with a disability rights orientation written by persons with first-hand experience. 16 Brighton Street, Rochester, NY, 14607.

Nagler, M. (1993). <u>Perspectives on disability</u>. 2nd Ed. Palo Alto, CA: Health Markets Research.

Prince B. Philips-Carmichael, I. & Shaner, K. F. (1993). <u>Individual technical training and placement program: The Accent Program at Hocking College</u>. Final report. Nelsonville, OH: Author.

Zuckerman, D., Debenham, K., & Moore, K. (1993). <u>The ADA and people with mental illness: A resource manual for employers</u>. Alexandria, VA: American Bar Association and the National Mental Health Association, 1993.

Situating Sexual Orientation on the Diversity Agenda:
Recent Legal, Social and Economic Developments

Key Points

The growing forces that are coalescing to make sexual orientation an important form of diversity for corporate attention are outlined.

Social Forces:

- Gays and their organizations have an increasingly public profile.

- Public attitudes are becoming more supportive.

Legal Forces:

- Gay rights laws have been enacted in over 80 U.S. cities with ordinances enacted in many more and 23 states have removed sodomy laws.

- Other countries have progressed even further than the U.S. on this issue.

Economic Forces:

- Gays are a lucrative consumer market.

- Gays are exerting economic pressure on gay-unfriendly companies.

Unions:

- Unions have adopted non-discriminatory clauses in contracts.

- Some unions are negotiating gay-specific issues.

Activism:

- Gay activist employee groups are emerging.

Answers to Discussion Questions
by Gerald Hunt

1. What factors or forces might continue to discourage some organizations from taking on the issue of gay and lesbian rights in the workplace? How might these factors or forces be overcome? Factors/forces:

- Too controversial

- Will cause problems

- Best let sleeping dogs be

- Will offend some people on basis of religious beliefs

61

- Do not want to be seen as leader in this area - best wait and see what other places do

- May offend some customers/clients

- We don't have any gays or lesbians here anyway

- Nobody has asked - lets wait until they ask

- It will cost too much money

- If we give them benefits, then we will have to give anyone who lives with anyone else, benefits too

- Not a priority - we have enough Human Resources Management problems as it is

- Isn't it still illegal? We can't be seen to support anything illegal

- Gay and lesbians chose their lifestyle and there are some costs associated with that choice

- They are not like other groups who are born with differences

Counter-arguments:

- Who decides one group is unequal and can be treated differently?

- May shift some gay and lesbian customers/clients/support in our direction

- Improve the job satisfaction, morale and motivation of our gay and lesbian employees - and will send a clear message that we are prepared to take on controversy when it comes to supporting diversity

- Lots of other places (Apple Computers, Lotus, Levi Strauss) have done this and they continue to prosper

- Many of the same sorts of arguments were used to keep other minorities and women from gaining equal rights - that didn't make it right, and it's not right for gays or lesbians either

- Either we value diversity or we don't - we can't arbitrarily exclude one group

- The vast majority of gays and lesbians report that they do not choose their sexual preference, it is just the way it is. Given the kind of hate that surrounds this group, why would anyone choose it? Besides, couldn't one say that religious beliefs are learned and chosen? We don't discriminate on the basis of religious beliefs, and welcome a variety of differing spiritual perspectives (Christians, Jews, Muslims, Agnostics, etc.)

- Gays and lesbians come in all shapes and sizes - just like other groups of people. You'll like some and not others (mention for example, that many politicians are openly gay, many people in the arts are gay, and that gays and lesbians are in every occupational group - at the same time, some are criminals and do not contribute to society - just like we find in the heterosexual population)

2. What suggestions do you have for designing an effective, in-house training program on diversity, one designed to incorporate gay and lesbian issues, along with gender and racial issues?

- Make sure gay and lesbians are involved in planning and teaching such a workshop. Use gay and lesbian community resources if no one inside the organization feels comfortable being involved

- Get advice from other organizations about what worked and what didn't

- Make sure the gay and lesbian parts are NOT just about AIDS

- Allow people to talk about their fears and discomforts, but in the end make sure people realize it is THEIR responsibility to work through diversity issues. Don't allow negative feelings about gays and lesbians to dominate and don't allow them to be legitimized as okay. If it is a hostile environment, speak for gays and lesbians who may be too frightened to speak for themselves.

- Expose the myths (for example, pedophilia or sexual attraction to children is a serious problem in society, but is quite distinct from being gay or lesbian or heterosexual)

- Make sure that all constituent groups involved in such a diversity workshop have time to plan the workshop and understand how they will work together (just because someone is a member of a minority group doesn't mean they will automatically be inclusive of other minorities, and there may be issues between various groups to get resolved before putting on the workshop in a public forum)

- IBM has some experience with diversity training that provides for a session on homophobia - find out what they did and how it worked

- Be sure to draw lots of parallels among the various groups – discrimination tends to operate in a similar manner, often deriving out of negative and misinformed stereotypes. Ultimately, prejudice is about ignorance and power, and that needs to be exposed and diffused

- May people claim they have never met a gay man or lesbian - make sure such a workshop gives them the opportunity to see one in the flesh and to realize they don't have two heads or claws

3. Put yourself in the position of a spokesperson for a gay and lesbian employee group in a medium–sized manufacturing company. What strategy and arguments would you use when presenting management with a proposal to include same-sex spousal benefits for such things as health insurance, bereavement leave, and company pension plans?

- See some of the arguments under Question 1

- Deal with issues under rubric of "do we really want to even try to justify discrimination?" In such an environment, is anyone really safe?

- The most effective strategy would probably include rational and political activities

- Get important people on your side; form coalitions

- Lobby inside and outside the organization

- Get someone from an organization that gives such benefits to give a talk

- Try to get clients/customers on your side if possible (for example, some cities and even some companies will actively try to support companies that have good coverage for minorities, including gays and lesbians

- Get info re what it would cost (usually very, very small amount of money)

- Try to find out how many people would take advantage of it

- Prepare a report indicating what places are already doing it, especially any places that are considered competitors (Lotus, for example, has had a lot published about their activities - see also references contained in the paper, especially the ones from Fortune and The New York Times

- Prepare a policy that will prevent any abuse of benefits (for example, how would gay and lesbian employees establish they were in an intimate and long-term partnership?)

SECTION III
Cases: *Instruction Notes and Answers to Discussion Questions*

Ticket Agent Fired over Makeup Policy
Continental Airline's Appearance Standards Policy

Instruction Notes
by William C. Sadd

Introduction

Continental Airlines was in serious financial difficulty in early 1991. Management was attempting to implement a number of diverse strategies aimed at cutting costs, increasing their passenger load factor, and restoring the airline to profitability.

One relatively small program dealt with improving the appearance of their passenger service personnel through the issuance of new uniforms and implementing conservative appearance standards for both men and women. Among the features of these standards was the requirement that women wear a minimum amount of make-up.

In the space of two months during that Spring, a part-time Customer Service Representative at Boston's Logan Airport - Teresa Fischette - single-handedly took on Continental and won. Defying their new policy, Teresa was fired, only to be re-hired with apologies several weeks later as Continental backed down and reversed their appearance standards policy.

Answers to Discussion Questions

1. Assess Continental's development of its new appearance standards. To what extent were the concepts of " diversity" and "otherness" applicable or incorporated into the process?

>   On the surface, Continental appeared to follow a very straight-forward process in developing the new policy. The employee-selected Employee Council and 16-person Professional Standards Committee were clearly representative of the employees. Almost half of its members (seven) were women who were the ones insisting that a minimum of make-up be included in the policy.

>   While we do not know the background and positions of these seven women, they may not have been truly representative of the women in field locations, and may have more closely associated themselves with corporate management. What may have seemed as a reasonable "make-up" policy may not have taken into consideration the reaction to the policy by field personnel. They also seem to have failed to have adequately considered the impact, if any, of make-up on their customer's perceptions of quality service.

>   There appeared to be a single-mindedness of focus on the new standards - the customer, without giving adequate consideration to the individuals upon whom the standards would be imposed.

>   Undoubtedly, the Committee failed to consider the possibility that there would be a ground-swell of protest against the new policy, much less from one person like Teresa.

2. Were there problems with Continental's appearance standards themselves, or with the way in which they were implemented? Identify changes in both which would have improved the likelihood of a successful implementation.

>   On the surface, the appearance standards appear to have been reasonable, part of a larger effort to improve the image of the airline and its customer service. Clearly, some standards are appropriate.

The main problem appears to have been in their implementation. When the new standard was introduced in March, 1991, it is not clear the extent of feedback that was either requested or received. Clearly, they received feedback from Teresa, and presumably others.

This represented a critical juncture for the Committee. Having committed themselves to the new standard, could they objectively assess the comments coming back and openly consider modifications to their standard that met corporate objectives (image, customer service, etc.) without the negative imposition on their employees?

3. Assess Teresa Fischette's relative power in this situation, relative to Continental, and identify the principal sources of this power.

On the surface, Continental clearly had the greater power. Their sheer size as a corporation, their financial resources (in spite of their bankrupt condition), their legitimate ability to define and impose reasonable working conditions on their employees, their ability to reward (or withhold rewards) from their employees, and their ultimate coercive power to punish, discipline or even fire an employee.

Teresa, on the surface, as a part-time Service Representative, had very little power or leverage. She was easily replaceable in her position. However, there were several fundamental factors that resulted in her having considerable power:

- She was skilled and experienced in various activist activities.

- She was highly principled and obviously persistent, prepared to keep this battle going until it was successfully resolved and she was vindicated.

- She had extensive personal contacts to advise her or point her to others who could help, and she knew or quickly learned of the groups (governmental and activist) to contact for assistance.

- Ultimately, it was her ability to build coalitions of groups, especially the media, starting with the Boston Globe articles, and culminating with the Oprah Winfrey and Jay Leno shows.

Continental was in a position to resist or ignore most of Teresa's efforts to have the policy changed, but they could not ignore the negative image damage resulting from the national media attention - with the likes of the Tonight Show skits. They had to cut their losses and give in to Teresa.

4. Assess Teresa's response to Continental's new policy. Why was she successful? What could she have done differently?

Teresa's response was reasonable, steady and persistent. She made every attempt to work the issue through channels at Continental, through a series of letters and personal visits. Having decided that the new standard was unreasonable, she was determined to see it changed, regardless of the effort required; it had become a matter of principle.

Her understanding and application of the trimtabbing technique (discussed below) helped her to identify Continental's vulnerability (i.e., negative national publicity), and her genuine desire was to avoid ugly public confrontation or embarrassment to Continental until it became apparent that such tactics were necessary.

In the end, she was successful for the reasons discussed in Question 3. It is hard to see many areas where she could have done things differently or more effectively.

5. Describe Teresa's use of the trimtabbing technique, citing specific examples, and assess its effectiveness and the reasons therefore.

> The real use of trimtabbing probably started on April 5 when Teresa realized that a confrontation might be inevitable and she contacted NOW, CLU of Mass, and other groups, laying the groundwork for eventual public pressure.
>
> At the same time, she sought to find "face-saving" alternatives by writing six letters to Continental and pulling together her monthly performance report cards.
>
> At the same time, she stepped up her "public-relations" campaign preparation with the visits to NOW and RESULTS in Washington, and arrangements for appearances on the national TV and print media.
>
> Overall, it was a well orchestrated campaign that steadily escalated until the eventful skit on the Tonight Show. Even if that skit had a lesser impact, other appearances were in the wings, ready to go.

6. Why did Continental reverse its position with such suddenness, making their mandatory appearance policy optional, after having been so adamant against changing it?

> Continental could not afford any more damage to its image through the negative publicity it was receiving. Even if the appearance standard had been a "good" strategic move, the cost had become too high.

7. Would the results of this case tend to help or hurt the position of other women employees at Continental, or in the workforce in general? Discuss.

> This is a complex question with no clear answer, but a number of possible ramifications for women at Continental and in the general workforce. While the overall results should be positive, there are some negative "back-lash" aspects which might be anticipated.
>
> At Continental, the reversal of the policy was clearly a victory for women, freeing them from arbitrary imposed standards. It shifted the focus more towards the quality of their job performance and less on what they looked like. It is also likely that improved consideration of the "diversity" and "otherness" of their workforce may result when new policies are being developed that have similar implications.
>
> However, the public's interest and attention quickly fades, and this may prove to be a short-term victory for women if future "discriminatory" practices are not effectively challenged when they are put forward.
>
> At the same time, there could well be a back-lash effect from some male managers who become more cautious and closed in their dealings with women, wondering who will be the next Teresa and where she may be hiding. Many men are uncomfortable with overly assertive and powerful women who can challenge their traditional authority and power. There may also be resentment for the forced reversal of what may have been viewed as a good policy.

Prologue

Teresa Fischette was re-hired by Continental Airlines on May 15, 1991, and continued to work for several months. In the Fall of 1991, she resigned, indicating that she had not been forced out, but acknowledging that there were some "problems" after she hit the media big time with Oprah Winfrey. At the time, she had no specific plans but wanted to get involved in grassroots organizing.

Al The Joker

Instruction Notes
by Robert P. Crowner and Jeannette Pryciak

Overview

Christy was disturbed and uncomfortable with the sexually explicit comments she was getting from Al, a well liked guy in her department at the A. C. Insurance Company. When she complained to the Human Resources department of the company, nothing was done. However, when news got back to her department that she had filed a complaint against Al for his behavior, the other employees were upset with her for reporting Al over nothing and told her that she overreacted.

Jackie, another girl in the department, knew that Christy was correct in her accusation against Al. Al had aimed his "jokes" Jackie's way many times. Jackie had talked to a friend in another department about the situation, but the advice she got from her friend was just to say nothing and avoid causing trouble.

Jackie was left with a big decision. Should she report Al, ignore him hoping he would go away, or leave the company?

Use of Case

This case can be used to show the insensitive behavior people sometimes show toward a victim, in this case a victim of sexual harassment. It also shows the way negative behavior by peers can affect a victim's judgment and decision.

Objectives of Case

The objectives are to make people aware of sexual harassment in the work place and how "jokes" of any sexual nature can be and are taken as sexual harassment. Also, it points out that the reactions of other people will not always be in support of the victim and in some cases will actually support the harasser. The case further illustrates the reluctance of management to pursue a sexual harassment allegation.

Analysis of Case

Problems: 1. Sexual harassment is being ignored by the company.

2. Harasser is not being reprimanded or even counseled.

3. Victim did not receive any support or help.

4. Victim received additional harassment from peers after she made a complaint.

5. Jackie, a second victim, was told that her job might be in jeopardy if she also complained.

6. Employees and management were not trained or informed about sexual harassment policy if indeed the company had one.

7. Jackie was left with a hard decision to make regarding Al without any positive guidance.

8. There was a breach of confidentiality by someone from the Human Resources department.

Observation

The case shows that A. C. Insurance Company may have poor, inadequate and/or nonexistent policies and procedures regarding handling of sexual harassment complaints. It also appears that employees and managers are ill informed on sexual harassment and how to handle such complaints.

Conclusions and Solutions

The company needs to create, update and/or codify its policies and procedures on sexual harassment. A training seminar should be conducted for management on how to identify, report and treat sexual harassment. An additional training seminar should be held for all employees on the subject to define sexual harassment, explain the policy and procedures, and the penalties. The definition should include improper jokes, language, and behavior. Reporting to the company and E.E.O.C. should be outlined.

Specific solutions should include the following.

1. Ensure all employees understand the severity of sexual harassment and that it must be taken seriously.

2. A confidential reporting system for employees should be established.

3. All incidents should be investigated.

4. A progressive system of corrective action should be established including counseling, reprimand, punishment and termination.

5. Company policies regarding sexual harassment should be prominently posted in employee areas so that employees are aware of them.

Preparation Suggestions

Students should note that this case took place in 1990 before the Thomas-Hill hearings which heightened the awareness of sexual harassment in the work place. Outside reading on the subject would be useful to bring students up to the current state of affairs.

Answers to Discussion Questions

1. Does this situation constitute sexual harassment? Why or why not?

    Yes, it is sexual harassment because it is unwelcome and distracting to Christy in terms of doing her job.

2. What was wrong with the way the company handled Christy's complaint?

    The company essentially did nothing. Al was not reprimanded and Christy was not helped.

3. What was wrong with the attitude of the other employees?

    They did not understand the severity of the harassment as Christy felt it. They even defended Al against the victim and in a sense furthered the harassment. Cheri, the supervisor, played favorites and did not take action against Al.

72

4. What was wrong with the advice received from her friend Sue?

>Sue advised her to keep quiet and thus caused her to continue to be a victim by influencing her to be afraid of losing her job.

5. What should Jackie do?

>Jackie should report Al to the company thus lending weight to Christy's complaint. If the company takes no action, she should report the situation to the E.E.O.C.

Subsequent Events

Jackie decided that at the time it was in her own best interests to try to ignore Al. She was able to get her desk moved to a different part of the department so she no longer had to sit next to him. Jackie was young and uninformed regarding her rights and did not want to deal with what Christy was going through. A few months later, Al received a job in another department which was an opportunity Al had been awaiting. The move had nothing to do with the complaint and, in effect, was made in spite of the complaint. Christy continued working for the company in the same job. Nothing was ever done by the company regarding her complaint.

Briarwood Industries

Instruction Notes
by Carol P. Harvey

This case can be used to illustrate to students that their gender affects their perceptions of a situation and that women and/or minorities are responsible for their own careers and should not rely on others to do their career planning for them. Assign the case to be read before students come to class. Female students who read this case, come to class prepared to defend Diane as a hardworking woman who has been passed over for a promotion. In contrast, male students see Diane as not being assertive enough about her career aspirations. Before beginning the case discussion, ask female students to sit on one side of the room and males on the other. Then ask them to turn their chairs toward the center of the room so that the two groups face each other.

To further reinforce their stereotypes about the genders, distribute an 8 1/2 by 11 inch sheet of pink paper to each male and a blue sheet to each female. Each student is to fold the sheet of paper into thirds, like a business letter, to form a name tent. Then ask each student to write their real first name on the middle third of the sheet and to place it in front of them like a placard. The purpose of the colored name tent is to remind the students that in this case discussion, men must speak from a female position, hence the pink name tent, and females from a male perspective, hence the blue name tent. At first students are stunned by this directive. When they begin to speak they feel a little silly but they soon get into the role reversals. The discussion rules are:

- Speak in a normal voice (no high pitched male voices etc.)

- Raise your hand to be called on

- If any student gets out of his/her role (males from a female perspective and females from a male perspective), the opposite group is simply to raise their hands as a reminder. This is why the two groups face each other.

  NOTE: Although you may have to remind students of this one or two times in the beginning of the class, they quickly get into their roles. It is important that the students, not the instructor, control this aspect of the discussion.

Now simply conduct a discussion of the Briarwood case. What usually happens during the case discussion is interesting and mirrors the findings of the American Association of University Women's study of male/female classroom behavior. The "males" (actually your female students), will usually speak first, speak more often, interrupt others and forget to raise their hands before speaking. The "females" (actually your male students), will take longer to get into the discussion, feel more awkward, etc..

After the case discussion is completed, process what has happened in terms of the dynamics of switching roles. Both males and females often say that they felt awkward at first but soon got into this exercise. Ask students

- What are the advantages of being forced to see a situation from an opposite viewpoint?

- What did they learn about the opposite gender by being forced to take that position?

- How can they apply what they have learned in this experience to organizations and management?

- What changes did they notice about their own behavior as a result of the role reversals?

Answers to Discussion Questions

1. Is Diane's reaction to Larry's promotion justified? Why or why not?

> While a case can be made that Diane is simply jealous of Larry's success, and disappointed at her own failure to get the job, the facts also indicate that she is a valuable employee with line experience and a viable track record at the company.

> It is also a possibility that she is up against a "glass ceiling" at Briarwood because she was not considered "corporate material". One would need to know how other women and minorities are represented at the highest levels of the organization to draw any valid conclusions.

> NOTE: As students get into their "roles" here, expect male students to defend Diane as the wronged employee and female students to say that she got what she deserved for being so passive.

2. Does Diane have legal grounds to sue the company?

> In regard to the promotion, it would be difficult to prove that Larry got the job because he was a man. He was qualified and also savvy about what it took to get ahead at Briarwood. In addition, there are no data given about how many other women are or are not in key management positions at the company.

> In regard to the $5,000 salary differential, she may have a case but this issue would have to be investigated further. Was she paid less because of her level of experience, the quality of her performance appraisals or are there real differences in how men and women are paid at the company?

3. Who is mainly at fault for this situation? Why?

> Both Diane and Gary share some blame for this situation. Gary failed to develop a good employee by not conducting career planning discussions with Diane. Diane assumed that if she worked hard, her efforts would be noticed and rewarded without her speaking up for herself and clearly asking for what she wanted in terms of her career moves.

> NOTE: With the role reversals expect males to defend Diane's behavior and females, Gary's. Female students will point out that Diane is a big girl who should by now know how the game is played. Her boss can not be expected to be a mind reader. In contrast, male students, if they really get into the role reversals, may point out that it is a manager's job, especially at that level, to do career planning with his employees. The organization rewarded Larry's grandstanding and punished Diane's less flamboyant style.

4. If Diane leaves Briarwood, what does she stand to lose? If she leaves, what will the company lose?

> Although Diane could probably easily get another job, she may carry with her a bitterness and sense of failure about her experience at Briarwood. If she continues to be passive in regard to her own career and as unaware of the politics of the new organization as she was of the old one, she may find herself in the same situation again. Ultimately, Diane stands to lose both self-esteem and a sense of pride in her accomplishments. If she leaves, the company will not only lose a valuable employee, but one on a high enough level to have knowledge that would be quite valuable to a competitor.

5. If you were Diane's best friend, Sandy, what advice would you give Diane about this situation?

> While students may say that a friend is a friend and will support you no matter what the facts are, others will say that the value of informal networks in a company lies in the ability to offer different perspectives and information. Sandy is in the position to offer advice only if Diane is open to hearing it and this does not appear to be the case here.

NOTE: For this question and Question 6, do not indicate in any way Sandy or Chris' gender, which is purposely not given in the case. Both names could be male or female. Be especially careful not to use any personal pronouns, etc. Many students will assume that Diane's friend is a woman and Gary's a man but there is no evidence for these conclusions in the case. This can trigger a rich discussion of the value of having close friends of the opposite gender who may offer a different perspective on a problem.

6. If you were Gary's best friend Chris, what advice would you give him about this situation?

In contrast to Diane, Gary seems to be eager for his friend's perspective on the problem. All we know from the case is that Chris has experience managing women, and this is considered a valuable commodity by Gary. Gary seems to think that there are special skills needed for managing women.

This provides an excellent opportunity to ask the women (who are really the males in the class), if they think that women need to be managed differently. Then ask the men (the females in the class), the same question: do men need to be managed differently? It may be necessary to remind students to stay in their reversed roles here, as the discussion usually gets quite heated about this issue.

7. What can Diane learn from this experience?

She needs to make her wants known, to put her personal issues on the table for open discussion or she will be passed over. The fact that she was aware of the salary differential and chose not to address it, does not indicate that she was very assertive about herself. In many ways she colluded with Gary by her passive behavior. Diane bears some of the responsibility for this situation because she did not bring her career aspirations and desire for this promotion to her boss's attention herself.

8. What can Gary learn from this experience?

It is the responsibility of managers, especially senior managers, to discuss performance and career issues in a straight forward way with their employees. A lack of addressing the fact that she was not considered "corporate material" with Diane, was a cowardly way out of the situation.

9. What are the lessons from this case for men and women working together in organizations?

The best lessons here are not learned from Diane and Gary's situation but from the experience of spending an hour or so being the opposite gender and having to see things from that perspective.

Ask the students to share their personal "lessons" from this experience and then apply these to the workplace. For example, the females in the class (the real ones) may mention that they felt it was all right here to interrupt to get into a conversation. This prompts a discussion of how difficult it may be for women to make themselves heard in a meeting, etc. Males (the real ones) in the class often mention that they felt that doing a good job just wasn't enough in this case. Relate that to the "glass ceiling" that many competent women experience in organizations, etc.

Freida Mae Jones

Instruction Notes
by Carol P. Harvey

This case, set in the late 1970's and early 80's, details the educational and employment experiences of an intelligent young black woman. As both the first female and the first black executive at the West Springfield branch of the Industrial World Bank of Boston, Freida feels that she is being treated differently than other employees by her boss, Stan Luboda.

Although the case presents no evidence that Freida is performing poorly, Luboda is not allowing her the same level of responsibility and experience as another trainee, Paul Cohen. When Freida brings this issue to Luboda's attention, he attributes her feelings to being overly sensitive about her race. Luboda presents the rationale that banking is a conservative, slowly changing business whose customers may not be ready to do business with a black female.

Major issues that need to be discussed about this case include: the roles and responsibilities of top management in implementing more successful EEO/AA programs; differences between whites' lack of awareness of the effects of their racial identity in contrast to that of blacks (see McIntosh); the costs of losing a highly intelligent employee after two years in a training program because of management's racist and sexist attitudes; the loss of the opportunity to obtain female and black customers who may feel more comfortable dealing with Freida than with a white male (see R. Roosevelt Thomas); and the risk of a lawsuit.

In addition, this case presents an excellent opportunity to discuss the events of the Civil Rights movement during this time period and its effect on both blacks and whites. Older students in the class who lived through that time of rapid change, will be able to share their experiences with students of traditional age, who may be less aware of the turmoil of those times.

Answers to Discussion Questions

1. Do you think that the Joneses' were being realistic or overly sensitive in their belief that their children would have to work harder to be successful because they were black? Explain your answer.

   > When anyone is in a minority position, their actions are more visible and more noticeable to others. This was especially true for blacks during the late 1960's and early 70's when the civil rights movement was rapidly changing American society. Although EEO/AA legislation opened some doors for minorities, it also put many of them in very visible positions with few support mechanisms. Many people were just waiting for a minority to fail because it presented an opportunity to point out than "we hired one and it didn't work out".

   > Consequently, the Jones' were probably quite realistic about their daughter's situation. Women often express this same sentiment.

2. If you were Freida, what else could you have done? If you were Mr. Luboda, what else could you have done?

   > Freida needed to help Luboda and others learn how to cope with the changes in the workforce. She needed to be more open with him on an ongoing basis instead of waiting for the situation to get intolerable. He may not have been aware of how differently he was treating her. As long as she went along with racist remarks etc., and indicated no displeasure, the white people at the bank may not have realized how offensive their actions were to Freida.

In addition, she needed to build her own support network. She could have kept in contact with the other black employees from her training program by telephone. They could have provided her with a good sounding board about interpreting events within her organization. She could also have attempted to find someone who worked at the bank who could mentor her in her career.

Luboda needed to educate himself about managing diverse employees. Minority and female professionals were a new phenomenon at the time of this case. Since Freida was both the first woman and the first black executive to work in the West Springfield branch, Luboda should have turned to the bank's human resources manager for advice on how to communicate more effectively with Freida.

3. Do you think that Luboda was discriminating against Freida? Why or Why not?

Luboda was treating Freida differently than Paul and that is discrimination. However, Luboda is probably acting as much out of ignorance as prejudice. He was probably as uncomfortable with her being female as he was with her being black.

Members of the majority culture are often unaware of how affected their behavior is by virtue of that membership. What Luboda considers good management, Freida sees as paternalism and racist/sexist behavior.

4. Does Freida have legal grounds to sue the bank for discrimination? Why or why not?

The 1964 Civil Rights Act states that it is illegal to limit, segregate, or classify employees or applicants for employment in any way which would deprive or tend to deprive any individual of employment opportunities or to otherwise adversely affect his status as an employee, because of such individual's race, color, religion, sex, or national origin.

There is no indication in this case that Freida's performance was poor but there is substantial evidence that she was highly educated and intelligent. This would put the bank in a very vulnerable legal position because she was not being offered the same opportunities as her co-worker.

5. What role did the bank's corporate management play in the managing diversity process? What could they have done differently?

The bank's corporate management seemed to have adopted a classical EEO stance. They may have hired minorities to fill a government quota but they did very little to help them succeed. The organization seemed to offer nothing in the way of support networks and in Freida's case the bank totally isolated her from the other minorities in her training group.

The bank also failed to provide Luboda, and probably other managers, with any training or support that helped them to learn how to deal with minority employees.

This would suggest that there was little serious top down support for diverse employees from the organization.

6. Luboda's arguments for his decisions about Freida's responsibilities seemed to be based on the idea that the bank's customers might be uncomfortable with a black female in a position of authority. Is this a valid argument? Why or why not?

This is neither a valid argument nor a legal one. The Springfield area had a growing black population in the late 1970's and early 80's. Since Freida was never given the opportunity to work directly with the customers, Luboda is probably using this argument to project his own discomfort with Freida's race and gender onto the customers.

In reality, there is little evidence that customers would refuse to deal with a bank that employed a black female executive. Having such an employee could even attract new customers to the bank.

Additional Resources

Bell, Ella Louise. (1990). The bicultural life experience of career-oriented Black women. <u>Journal of Organizational Behavior</u>, 11, 459-477.

Bell, Ella Louise. (1988-1989). Racial and ethnic diversity: The void in management education. <u>The Organizational Behavior Teaching Review</u>, 13, (4), 56 - 57.

Betters-Reed, B.L., & Moore, L.L. (1988-1989). Managing diversity in organizations: Racial and ethnic diversity: Professional and curricular issues. <u>The Organizational Behavior Teaching Review</u>, 13(4), 25-32.

Braham, Jim, "No, You Don't Manage Everyone the Same," <u>Industry Week</u>, February 6, 1989, pp. 28-30, 34-34.

Davis, George & Greg Watson. (1982). <u>Black life in corporate America</u>. Garden City, New York:Doubleday.

Fernandez, John. (1981). <u>Racism and sexism in corporate life</u>. Lexington MA:Lexington Books.

Foeman, A. K. & Pressley, G. (1987). Ethnic culture and corporate culture: Using Black styles in organizations. <u>Communications Quarterly</u>, 35, 293-307.

Kanter, Rosabeth Moss. (1977). Some effects of proportions on group life: Skewed sex ratios and responses to token women. <u>American Journal of Sociology</u>, 832(5), 965-990.

Katz, P.A. & Taylor, D.A. (1988). <u>Eliminating racism: Profiles in controversy</u>. New York: Plenum Press.

Mai-Dalton, R. (1984-1985). Exposing business students to cultural diversity: Becoming a minority. <u>The Organizational Behavior Teaching Review</u>, 9(3), 76-82.

Nkomo, Stella. (1992). The emperor has no clothes: Rewriting race in organizations. <u>Academy of Management Review</u>, 17, 487-513.

Solomon, Julie, "Firms Address Workers' Cultural Variety" The Differences are Celebrated, Not Suppressed", <u>Wall Street Journal</u>, February 10, 1989, pp. 5-6.

Thomas R. Roosevelt, Jr. ."From Affirmative Action to Affirming Diversity," <u>Harvard Business Review</u>, Mar/Apr 1990, 68:2, pp. 107-117.

Thomas R. Roosevelt, Jr. (1991). <u>Beyond race and gender: Unleashing the power of your total workforce by managing diversity</u> . New York:AMACOM.

The Emanuel Company

Instruction Notes
by Carole Copeland Thomas

Few small businesses have successfully reached the level of achievement of The Emanuel Company regardless of race or ethnicity. Don Emanuel's rich career background, ease of getting financing and strong client base make this case an intriguing one for students to comprehend the complexities of managing and operating a minority firm that fights to gain a foothold in a traditionally racially biased industry.

The case also includes distinctive incidents where race provided opportunities as well as extreme challenges for Don Emanuel. The impact of his physical characteristics and how he used his appearance is of particular note in this case, since the ramification of the lightness of one's skin color is rarely addressed in other business cases. The dilemma of affirmative action is also addressed in this case and how it worked both for and against the growth and development of The Emanuel Company.

Of particular note is how Don Emanuel was able to leave and re-enter an industry known for fierce competition and repeated business failures. To go off to explore the world through travel and personal development is a dream many have, but few people can act upon. To then re-open a company after satisfying that need is even rarer.

The Emanuel Company is a case richly mixed with business issues, diversity challenges and the quest of entrepreneurial excellence for one African American man. It spans a thirty year time period, highlights the economic ebbs and flows of Detroit, Michigan and reflects on the opportunity gains that resulted from the struggles of the civil rights movement.

Answers to Discussion Questions

1. How did race and Don's physical characteristics help his business pursuits? How did they add obstacles to his career and entrepreneurial path?

> One of the most pivotal events dealing with race and physical features affecting Don Emanuel was the Allen Park Restaurant incident that occurred during his Walbridge years (Race and the Walbridge Years 1965-1973). Don's ability to pass for a white man with his fair skin, keen facial features and wavy hair worked both for and against him during this incident. Located in an all white Detroit suburb, it was easy for him to be admitted and comfortably seated with his company colleagues and business guests. However, by allowing the assumption that he was ethnically "one of them" to go unquestioned, Don painfully found himself a victim of the off color jokes that were being presented as well. It was at that point that the game of race became too uncomfortable for him and his company colleagues to play.

> It is a well-known but frequently undiscussed phenomenon in the black community that lighter gradations of color often represent higher status levels within many social and economic circles. Lighter-skinned blacks are perceived by many as having more value than their darker skinned counterparts. This become a very sensitive issue within family groups, where some members are lighter than others. From the complex circumstances of slavery in the United States and the millions of off-spring of plantation owners and slave women have come generations of mixed blood African-Americans - many of whom are so light that they have been able to "pass" as white people to better their socio-economic status in life. It is this legacy of the hierarchy of color that allowed Don Emanuel to routinely leverage his appearance in business opportunities both in Detroit and Buffalo. (For Further information, read *The Color Complex* by Kathy Russell, Doubleday, 1992).

2. What affirmative action issues confront businesses like The Emanuel Company? Is affirmative action (AA) seen as a positive or negative enforcement, or both?

This is a difficult and complex question to answer, given the size and influence of The Emanuel Company. Yes, the firm did prosper because of AA, having originally started in the early 1970's when many companies were formally disbanding their discriminatory policies due to new government regulations and the years of struggles in the civil rights movement. At one time of its existence as a $12 million business, The Emanuel Company could easily bid on, win and complete major construction projects just like any small to mid-size white firms. They had a strong customer base, including Fortune 500 clients like The Ford Motor Company. By moving beyond the normal presumptions and expectations of many minority businesses - struggling, undercapitalized, poorly managed, minimal strategic plan, weak client base, etc. The Emanuel Company became less dependent on the original intent of AA that enforced and promoted non-discriminatory, open, honest and fair business practices.

One frustrating project that illustrated this dilemma was the $15 million Epcot Center venture (Future Growth of The Emanuel Company and Affirmative Action). The double-edge sword for Don Emanuel was knowing that his company could handle the entire project alone, only to realize that it was merely designed to be parceled out to several minority businesses. This more favorably positioned the Disney project as pro AA, by using many minority firms competing for smaller dollars instead of just one.

3. What role did John Rakolta, Sr. have in Don's life? Is that role a critical factor in why Don became an entrepreneur? What may have happened if there had been no intercom incident?

John Rakolta, Sr. began as an employer of Don Emanuel and eventually evolved into a mentor and ultimately a business partner. By giving Don the opportunity of succeeding at Walbridge by providing countless projects for him to manage, Rakolta helped to unlock Don Emanuel's door of achievement in the racially biased construction industry. Yes, Don Emanuel had the intellect, ability, talent, determination and commitment to achieve; however gaining favorable status with the company owner added significant value to the success of his career/entrepreneurial path. It especially proved favorable when Emanuel relaunched his business and was partially able to finance it due to Rakolta's investment.

The intercom incident was maliciously designed to hurt Don, but turned out to be one of the best things to happen to his career. It showed Emanuel's skill under pressure, solving problems with the resources he had at hand. Without an opportunity for Don to "prove himself under fire" his career might have been stunted.

4. What gender issues may occur in the relaunched Emanuel Company, given the growing number of women entering non-traditional industries in this country?

Accepting women as "equal players" will be an important issue/challenge facing The Emanuel Company. Traditional perceptions of women being "the weaker sex" may negatively influence how women are treated as laborers, project managers and office administrators as The Emanuel Company grows. Don's personal views of women and their importance within the construction industry will also weigh heavily on how successfully they are represented in his company. The impact of new sexual harassment guidelines will also influence how women progress in industry.

5. What are some issues facing The Emanuel Company in the future given an uncertain economic climate? How can the company leverage its strengths by pursuing alternative business opportunities in the future?

Issues include the following:

- Finding additional capital for business expansion

- Staffing/Human Resource/personnel changes and conflicts

- Changing role of unions in Michigan construction projects

- An unchanging/sluggish economy

- Don Emanuel's changing interest...will business remain an intense priority for him?

One important way The Emanuel Company can leverage its success is by developing a strong marketing strategy that visibly positions the firm as a forward-thinking, vision-oriented construction firm that is closely tied with the African-American community.

General Dynamics in the Navajo Nation
by Fairlee E. Winfield

Teaching Objectives of Notes

- To provide background material for the case study "General Dynamics in the Navajo Nation."

- To initiate the notion of social responsibility of U.S. industry toward the Native American Indian labor force.

- To introduce opportunities for private industry operations on sovereign American Indian Nation lands.

- To present an alternative to off-shore production.

- To increase awareness of an existing Native American Indian labor force.

Teaching Objectives of Case

- To consider the social responsibility of U.S. industry to the Native American Indian labor force.

- To introduce the concept of diversity in work related attitudes.

- To introduce the concept of "cultural synergy" in the management of a diverse work force.

- To recognize that societal environments differ widely even within the United States.

- To explore the strengths and weaknesses of an organization operating in a culturally diverse environment.

- To explore opportunities and threats present in the external environment of a culturally different society.

- To explore whether past performance in this culturally different domestic environment warrants expansion.

Use of Note and Case

This case is not intended to illustrate good or bad management. It is useful as an Organizational Behavior, Business Ethics, or Human Resources Management teaching tool to present the problems of social responsibility and the dilemmas of managing cultural diversity. The case has been used successfully in International Management senior level classes to clarify value system differences. Use in American Indian economic development seminars is suggested.

The Note introduces the case "General Dynamics in the Navajo Nation" and can be given to students before the case to provide the necessary background for case analysis, or it can be used separately to present the notion of social responsibility of U.S. industry toward the Native American Indian labor force.

The management awareness activity is designed to increase students' sensitivity to cultural diversity and to cross-cultural management dilemmas. The test of the management knowledge in the traditional Navajo American Indian culture sets the stage for both the Note and the Case by deliberately increasing the students' level of discomfort and anxiety. It is found in Section V of the text.

A set of questions is provided to accompany the Case. Both the Note and the Case can be covered in two 75 minute class periods, three 50 minute periods, or one 2 and 1/2 hour period. The Note or the Case could be used in isolation, but it is recommended that the analysis activity be included.

General Dynamics in the Navajo Nation

Overview

Mike Enfield, General Dynamics plant manager at the Fort Defiance, Arizona facility, was convinced that his Navajo American Indian employees were the tops. Nevertheless, he wondered whether General Dynamics should continue with lengthy negotiations for expansion and for a second facility in the Navajo Nation. In 1984, after 16 years of successful operation, General Dynamics wanted to enlarge the Fort Defiance facility by 15,000 square feet. The company also wanted to sign a new 20-year lease with the Navajo Tribal Council. Operations at the facility required adjustment to the customs of the Navajo host culture, and although it was a domestic setting, business was conducted as if it were a foreign environment. Quality was high, but so was absenteeism. There was a large labor pool, but training centers were lacking. Non-Indian employees had difficulty obtaining housing and medical services. Negotiations with the Navajo Tribal Council and the Bureau of Indian Affairs could go on for years. The tribal chairman, Peter MacDonald, had his own objectives spelled out in a 10-year Plan for Economic Development. The tone of this plan was clearly hostile to outsiders. How could barriers be removed and opportunities for both the Navajo Nation and General Dynamics continue to expand?

Suggested Teaching Approach

The case presents problems in management of cultural diversity and the dilemma of ethical considerations versus economic considerations. Administration of the "Test of Management Knowledge in the Traditional Navajo American Indian Culture" (see Chapter V) prior to use or discussion of the case simulates the discomfort associated with xenophobic responses and ethnocentricity. Teachers should emphasize the social responsibility of organizations operating on American Indian Tribal lands and the question of what the policy of U.S. industry should be towards the 1.4 million American Indian labor force. Use of the Note prior to the case sets the stage for considering the federal government's position supporting economic development programs in foreign countries under the Overseas Private Investment Corporation while this same support is not available to American Indian nations.

The case is appropriate in International business courses to alert students to the notion that you need not be on foreign soil to encounter a situation requiring cultural awareness and the need for cultural synergy. Cultural differences, both domestic and foreign, can lead to mutual growth and greater accomplishment, but there is also the possibility of alienation from the home culture and the home organization. The question of whether Enfield is highly sensitive to and appreciative of the Navajo culture or totally alienated from mainstream U.S. culture is of interest. If he is alienated, can he successfully represent General Dynamics interests?

The case has been well received by Navajo Indian students in the College of Business Administration at Northern Arizona University. It would be useful in all regions of the United States where Indian Nations, with their extremely complex tribal government systems, are encountering the dilemmas of economic development.

Note: Private Industry on American Indian Reservations

Overview

The Native American Indian labor force numbers 1.4 million. Anywhere from 30 to 80 percent of these Americans are unemployed. One federal government solution to American Indian unemployment required r*elocation of* Indian people to urban centers where they would be assimilated into the dominant Anglo/European culture. Next, American

Indians were to engage in agriculture and raise cattle and sheep. Now, the tribes themselves are trying casino gambling. The Note provides environmental and cultural background information to prepare students and seminar participants for the exploration of an alternative solution to offshore production - private industry manufacturing operations on Indian lands. It serves to set the stage for the case "General Dynamics in the Navajo Nation."

The Indian Nations are politically stable and have access to a well developed infrastructure. American Indian people have a well-developed work ethic and benefits accrue to corporations through Federal Government programs which fully fund training programs. Historical and social factors make it necessary to conduct operations with sensitivity to cultural values and traditions. Potential advantages are there for both industry and the Indian tribes.

Suggested Teaching Approach

The Note initiates the idea of social responsibility of U.S. private industry toward the Native American Indian labor force. Additionally, it presents an alternative solution to offshore production. Discussion might begin with the controversy over exporting jobs to Mexico and the Far East because of abundant, low-cost labor supply and move into the notion of alternatives. The idea of a reliable labor source available in American Indian Nations may be overlooked by students. Students may want to consider the casino gambling alternative. Is it more appropriate than private industry development?

Answers to Case Questions

1. What opportunities and advantages are present for general dynamics in the Navajo nation external environment?

    a. There is a large available labor pool with a skilled crafts tradition and high manual dexterity.

    b. Low labor costs begin at minimum wage. The product is high quality and very little quality control is needed.

    c. There is an affirmative action advantage from employment of Native American Indians.

    d. Costs are also kept down because of low turnover rates and high employee productivity.

    e. The ability of Navajos to assume leadership responsibility provides an opportunity to increase Navajo participation in the management of the facility.

    f. Private industry operating in the Navajo Nations has the opportunity to demonstrate social responsibility by contributing to American Indian economic development. This in turn generates a favorable public image and a sense of pride on the part of employees who are instrumental in the success of the operation.

    g. A favorable financial arrangement is made with the Tribe including availability of state and federal training funds which lower labor costs.

    h. The facility is designed, built, and equipped by the Navajo Tribal Council to meet company specifications creating an attractive financial arrangement with low initial capitalization cost.

    i. The Navajo Nation has good, reliable transportation and communication.

    j. Although the Navajo language is spoken by most people on the Reservation, English is taught in the schools and spoken widely in the domestic environment.

    k. A domestic setting is a requirement for corporations involved in the military weapons industry where information on product, production, and process is generally classified.

2. What threats and disadvantages are present for general dynamics in the Navajo nation external environment?

     a. Management must adjust to the customs of the host culture just as it would have to do in an international setting. This requires study of and interest in the Navajo culture. It also requires adequate and costly pre-deployment briefings of non-Indian employees. Assignment to the Navajo facility holds all the potential pitfalls of assignment to a foreign country including culture shock, inability of the family to adjust, anxiety, somatization of emotions, sojourner paranoia, disconfirmed expectancies, high ambiguity, prejudice and ethnocentrism, and finally reentry shock on return to the mainstream corporation.

     b. High absenteeism can be a problem. For example, the Navajo healing ceremony lasts nine days and tradition requires attendance. Therefore, overstaffing is necessary to avoid large fluctuations. Generally the work force is unaccustomed to coming to work every scheduled work day.

     c. The high rate of alcoholism on the Navajo Nation contributes to high absenteeism and can be a negative safety factor.

     d. The limited housing for both Navajo employees and non-Indian personnel threatens retention rates for both.

     e. Medical facilities are only available to Navajos. Non-Indian employees must travel 35 miles to Gallup, New Mexico even for emergencies.

     f. Negotiating with the tribal government is frustrating and time consuming. Tribal elections can mean that contract negotiations must begin all over. A new tribal government has no obligation to honor previous commitments.

     g. Political risk should be assessed before locating on sovereign American Indian Nations. The American Indian Movement is no longer as radically confrontational as in the 1970's. (Some students may mention the 1975 Fairchild plant takeover on the Navajo Nation.) Industry going off-shore accepts the political risks of locating in China, Korea, Mexico, and the Middle East. Political shifts in tribal government can affect operations.

3. As a general dynamics manager, how do you react to Tribal Chairman Peter MacDonald's objectives in the 10-year plan?

     The tone of MacDonald's objectives is that of intense Navajo nationalism. He views the American Indian situation as requiring both geographical and cultural separation. A history of exploitation, deprivation, and violation of government treaties leads to these statements. This same philosophy is seen in foreign nations like Mexico or Peru that attempt to create their own well-being from within. MacDonald is proposing isolationism as a solution to economic problems. The federal government has created a burdensome bureaucracy which has become institutionalized over a two-hundred year period. Indian Nations have lost their autonomy. They do not even receive economic development benefits available to foreign countries under the Overseas Private Investment Corporation.

     A responsible corporate response is to consider the General Dynamics-Navajo Nation relationship as a mutually supportive partnership, essentially "international" in context if not in law. As a General Dynamics manager you honor the partnership through your respect for Navajo culture and traditions. The partnership requires that you train Navajo employees for leadership and for management positions. Initially the plant had a management team of 26 non-Navajos. This number was reduced to seven by 1984.

MacDonald's statements could be threatening to new industry seeking to locate on tribal lands, but your partnership has shown its good faith over 16 years. Your position is sound and stable. The Navajo Tribe receives lease income for the plant facility, and the facility itself will remain in good condition if General Dynamics should decide to leave. In providing salaries for 320 employees, General Dynamics is creating an economic base from which there will be a multiplier effect. Navajo small business and service industry profit from these salaries.

4. What is the General Dynamics cultural position on important management strategies, policies, and programs?

The strategy of General Dynamics has been to consider the Navajo Nation operation as an international situation. The approach is similar to responsible corporate approaches to "underdeveloped" sovereign nations. This entails respect for the Navajo traditions and culture. The following examples of programs and policies can be cited.

- Plant dedication ceremony according to Navajo tradition.

- Screening of potential non-Indian managers and an on-site visit by the family to determine if the candidate and family can tolerate, and perhaps enjoy, being part of a local minority group.

- Over-staffing for high absenteeism that allows Navajo employees to participate in traditional religious and social ceremonies.

- Training of Navajo employees to assume leadership and management positions.

- A thorough but sensitive training and orientation program for new Navajo employees.

- Efforts to improve other aspects of life on the Navajo Nations such as: housing, health care, child care, continuing education facilities.

- Good faith and honest dealings with all members of the Navajo tribe.

5. Are there differences between non-indian and Navajo work related attitudes? Reference quotations in the case and in the technical note. Consider any of Geert Hofstede's dimensions.

Power Distance

Navajo employees do not accept that their boss has more power than they have or that their boss is right simply because he or she is the boss. The Navajo system is not based upon hierarchical relationships, but is egalitarian. Therefore, it would be rated as a low power distance on Hofstede's power distance dimension. Note that Enfield states, "You can not intimidate them." The U.S. system though ranked relatively low on power distance accepts the authority of a leader-boss. Meanwhile, the Navajo systems accepts the nurturing of a leader-father.

Individualism/Collectivism

Harmony is of great importance to the Navajo. Group decisions are preferred and community comes before self. Decision is by consensus. Social frameworks distinguish between clans, and people expect in-groups to look after their members, protect them, and give them security. The leader is a member of the group with nurturing, protective responsibilities. U.S. attitudes center on high individualism. The notion is to "do what is best for me."

Uncertainty Avoidance

The Navajo has a high tolerance for ambiguity. The culture is adaptive. Formal rules are minimal with a wait and see attitude that tolerates cognitive dissonance. These cultural views are strengthened by an unemployment rate of 33% (in some areas up to 80%) and centuries of broken treaties. The Navajo is highly risk tolerant. Governments and jobs may come and go; the people manage to survive. This risk tolerance is demonstrated in the inability to intimidate by threat of job loss or fines.

Masculinity/Femininity

Hofstede describes this dimension of work related behavior as follows: (1) Masculinity is the extent to which the dominant values in a society emphasize assertiveness and the acquisition of material things, (2) Femininity is the extent to which the dominant values in a society emphasize relationships among people. Avoid the notion that this dimension is related to the acceptance or rejection of women in the work force. The Navajo culture places greater value on relationships among people than on assertiveness. Therefore, it would be described as at least moderately feminine. Additionally, gender roles are not highly defined in the Navajo culture. When a job is to be done, whoever is available undertakes the task. Women hold leadership in the tribe and are the owners of property. Although the traditional agrarian culture is low-materialistic, Navajos place high value on the ownership of sheep and other livestock. Enfield notes that women are taking leadership positions in the plant.

Temporality

Time is not measured by minutes and hours; it is measured by a task to be accomplished. Notions of "on-time, in-time, my-time," are foreign to the traditional Navajo culture. The situation is like that encountered while doing business in Mexico or the Bahamas. Navajo people are present-oriented. To a large extent what they feel like doing on a particular day dictates what they will actually do. Nevertheless, employees meet plant production allotments.

Decision Making

Slow consensus decisions provide time for input by all group members and subsequent fast implementation. This contrasts with typical fast, top-down decision making in many U.S. corporations. The Navajo site lease negotiating process, sometimes lasting for years, is an extreme example of slow decision making.

6. Is there an emerging or well-defined cultural synergy composed of shared beliefs, expectations, and values that has defined past performance and that will probably affect future performance?

Cultural synergy, the behavior of the Navajo-General Dynamics partnership as a whole rather than two separate entities, is based upon mutual trust that has developed over a long time. Shared beliefs, expectations, and values have developed during this long term relationship. Culturally synergistic organizations like the Navajo-General Dynamics partnership create new forms of management and organization that transcend the individual cultures of the two groups. The central figure is the nurturing leader-father rather than the leader-boss. One aspect of this new form of management is the high value placed on quality by both employees and management. General Dynamics states that almost no "quality control" is needed.

7. As a General Dynamics manager, would you continue to pursue expansion in the Navajo nation? If so, what concessions might you try to get from the Navajo tribal council? (See below for actual situation.)

Concessions should involve housing, medical facilities, and training. Even Enfield feels there is some discrimination against non-Indian personnel since none of these facilities are available to them. However, most important is some speeding up of the lease negotiation process. Even pressure for restructuring the tribal government might be considered. The U.S. Bureau of Indian Affairs impedes development by adding additional bureaucratic requirements that could be reduced. The Overseas Private Investment Corporation could extend its programs to Indian Nations.

8. As tribal chair of the Navajo nation, would you want to pursue additional manufacturing opportunities with private industry? If not, what other means of economic development would you seek?

> A tribal chair may view private industry as merely exploiting the large labor pool while paying low wages. Or, manufacturing could be seen as providing an economic base for further development of the Navajo economy. People are being trained for skilled jobs and a few are learning management skills. An alternative for economic development might be small businesses developed by American Indian entrepreneurs.

9. Negotiating Perspective

> Responses here will vary depending on how participants view their own system and their partner's. Groups may or may not be ready to acknowledge a different stakeholder's perspective. Business people usually select negotiation when the following situations exist. Their power is low as compared to their negotiating partner's. (The General Dynamics group may see themselves as having greater power, or the Navajo group may feel they have more power.) Negotiation is selected when the trust level is high. (It is likely that the Navajo group has little trust in the white man's private company.) Also need for negotiation is available time to explore the needs, resources, and options of both parties. Commitment is important to ensure implementation. Negotiation is generally the preferred strategy for creating a win win- solution. However, a take-it-or-leave-it strategy is sometimes appropriate. Discuss whether or not it would be ethical in this case.

Answers to Analysis Activity

1. What are the advantages of locating on native American Indian lands?

Economic and ethical advantages exist, including:

   a. Abundant labor pool

   b. High quality of the labor pool

   c. Ability to train employees for complicated assembly

   d. High education level of labor pool

   e. Political stability

   f. Developed infrastructure

   g. Favorable financial arrangements h. Participation in American Indian economic development

   i. Pride in corporate social responsibility

2. What are the disadvantages of locating on native American Indian lands?

International nature of the operation creates negotiation of cultural disadvantages, including:

   a. Cultural and traditional considerations: values, attitudes, behaviors of labor force

   b. Acculturation problems for non-Indian employees

   c. Difficulty in negotiation with tribal governments

93

d. Difficulty in negotiation with Bureau of Indian Affairs

e. Difficulty with archeological and environmental clearance

f. Overcoming stereotypes of "Indians" (students may mention images derived from films that either idealize or vilify American Indian people)

g. Time needed for site leasing

Group Two: American Indian Nation Economic Development Committee

1. What are the advantages of attracting private industry to locate on your sovereign lands?

   Economic and social advantages exist, including:

   a. Reduce high unemployment

   b. Decrease reliance on government jobs

   c. Multiplier effect can create opportunity for local American Indian owned businesses

   d. Stop movement of young people away from Indian lands

   e. Alleviation of peripheral problems brought on by unemployment (alcoholism, low self-image, lack of goals)

   f. Improved training and educational opportunities

2. What are the disadvantages of private industry locating on your sovereign lands?

   a. Past experience with "white traders" poor

   b. Need to adapt Indian culture and values

   c. Possible loss of native language and cultural identity

   d. Exploitation of labor force

   e. Only "whites" allowed in management positions f. Autonomy further threatened by corporations g. Potential for destruction of environment

Then discuss what the U.S. Industry policy should be towards the 1.4 million Native American Indian labor force, - the nation's oldest minority group.

Epilogue

Negotiations with the Navajo Tribal council for a 20-year lease extension and expansion of the Fort Defiance, Arizona facility were completed in late 1984 under Peterson Zah who was then tribal chairman. In 1990, a second General Dynamics facility was opened outside Farmington, New Mexico on the Navajo Agricultural Products Industries (NAPI) land. The new facility opened with only three non-Indian employees. A forthcoming case study will document development of the Farmington General Dynamics facility. Over the past fifteen years, General Dynamics management has frequently acted as an advocate for investment by industry on American Indian Nations. By speaking from experience the corporation can realistically present both advantages and disadvantages at seminars on American Indian economic development.

In late 1992 as part of the Hughes takeover of General Dynamics, the Navajo Facility at Fort Defiance became part of Hughes Missile Systems. The Facility continues to operate profitably and successfully on the Navajo Nation in 1993.

Mike Enfield is still at the Fort Defiance facility. He is now in charge of Human Resources and External Affairs for the Hughes' Navajo Operations which include both facilities. He works closely with the Tribal Council that is undertaking a major restructuring of the tribal government with the notion of facilitating economic development. The federal government appears to be cooperating.

As this case goes to press, the Navajo Tribe is considering establishing casino gambling enterprises along Interstate Highways I-40 at Leupp, Arizona. Meanwhile, the State of Arizona has expressed annoyance with Tribal casinos by confiscating gambling equipment from the Fort McDowell Indian Reservation casinos near Phoenix. Both Navajo Nation Facilities are actively seeking contracts outside the lagging defense industry.

Notes

1. Theoretical discussion of the issues in this case are contained in the following: (1) Nancy J. Adler, International Dimensions of Organizational Behavior, Second Edition, PWS-Kent Publishing Co., Boston, 1991, Chapters 1-7; (2) Geert Hofstede, Culture's Consequences: International Differences in Work Related Values, Sage Publications, Beverly Hills, 1980.

2. Geert Hofstede, "Motivation, Leadership, and Organizations: Do American Theories Apply Abroad?" Organizational Dynamics, Summer 1980, pp. 42-63.

Mail Management Systems: *The Karin Hazam Case*

by Becky DiBiasio

This case examines Karin Hazam's remarkable achievements as a deaf, female business owner and the development of her company which was formed to employ disabled workers. MMS is an example of how a determined and savvy CEO managed diversity in her workforce and her product line and turned perceived disabilities into assets while achieving economic growth.

Teaching Objectives

- To describe how Karin Hazam turned a handicap into an advantage and economic asset and used her own background as a training ground for employing physically challenged workers.

- To describe how she used networking skills (in particular, her work with the Carter Administration and the Navy) to expand her company.

- To explain how Karin Hazam was able to develop sales advantages by becoming an expert in laws regarding small business ownership, handicaps and gender.

- To explore the ramifications of Karin's management style. She controls every aspect of the business, from sales to job training; this is both an advantage and a limitation to growth.

Instruction Notes

Karin Hazam overcame a physical disability - deafness, and zeroed in on the necessity for businesses to accommodate disabled workers. Using her own experiences in overcoming prejudice and coping with the lack of jobs and facilities for physically challenged workers, she built an organization that depends on managing diversity within a predominantly disabled workforce (80% of her employees are disabled). How did she accomplish this?

Karin Hazam envisioned MMS as 1) a place to train and employ disabled workers and 2) a successful business. She concentrated on bidding for non-primary jobs such as packaging, mailing, shipping and recycling, knowing that most businesses would rather contract these jobs to independents than expand space and employees on secondary work. Beginning with bulk mailing jobs, she used contacts she had make in her own struggles to achieve job equality in order to develop a company with a strong market base. Among other things, she consolidated jobs whenever possible and trained each worker to perform several jobs. In particular, she relied on her knowledge of business laws affecting women and handicapped workers and employers.

She utilized every tax credit advantage that she could find. For instance, she has relied heavily on the IRS Disabled Access Tax Credit, which reads as follows:

This new tax credit is available to "eligible small businesses" in the amount of 50 percent of "eligible access expenditures" that exceed $250 but do not exceed $10,250 for a taxable year. A business may take the credit each year that it makes an eligible access expenditure.

Eligible small businesses are those businesses with either:

- $1 million or less in gross receipts for the preceding tax year; or

- 30 or fewer full-time employees during the preceding tax year.

Eligible access expenditures are amounts paid or incurred by an eligible small business for the purpose of enabling the business to comply with the applicable requirements of the Americans with Disabilities Act (ADA). These include amounts paid or incurred to:

- remove architectural, communication, physical, or transportation barriers that prevent a business from being accessible to, or usable by, individuals with disabilities;

- provide qualified readers, taped texts, and other effective methods of making orally delivered materials available to individuals with hearing impairments;

- provide qualified interpreters of other effective methods of making orally delivered materials available to individuals with hearing impairments;

- acquire or modify equipment or devices for individuals with disabilities; or

- provide other similar services, modifications, materials or equipment.

Expenditures that are not necessary to accomplish the above purposes are not eligible. Expenses in connection with new construction are not eligible. "Disability" has the same meaning as it does in the ADA. To be eligible for the tax credit, barrier removals or the provision of services, modifications, materials or equipment must meet technical standards of the ADA Accessibility Guidelines where applicable. These standards are incorporated in the Department of Justice regulations implementing Title III of the ADA (28 CFR Part 36; 56 CFR 35544, July 26, 1991).

Example

Company A purchases equipment to meet its reasonable accommodation obligation under the ADA for $8,000. The amount by which $8,000 exceeds $250 is $7,750. Fifty percent of $7,750 is $3,875. Company A may take a tax credit of $3,875 on its next tax return.

Example

Company B removes a physical barrier in accordance with its reasonable accommodation obligation under the ADA. The barrier removal meets the ADA Accessibility Guidelines. The company spends $12,000 on this modification. The amount by which $12,000 exceeds $250 but not $10,250 is $10,000. Fifty percent of $10,000 is $5,000. Company B is eligible for a $5,000 tax credit on its next tax return. (Disabled Access Tax Credit, Title 26, Internal Revenue Code, Section 44)

Given the ramifications of this code, large companies may receive tax credits for buying specialized equipment for Karin's company. MMS is already handicapped accessible, so the large companies receive a tax credit for providing equipment while MMS provides the accessible facility.

This, plus Small Business Administration Certification and advantages for women owners of small businesses, in addition to the wide-ranging tax breaks available through the ADA, have given her clear advantages over her competitors.

She has also succeeded by keeping her priorities intact. Although she has expanded her company considerably over the past five years, she does not intend further expansion in the near future. She is planning to consolidate and concentrate more rigorously on training programs and on providing independent living quarters for her workers.

This highlights one potential problem area for MMS. One important management skill is to understand every level of one's business, but one disadvantage for Karin is that everyone who works for her is reliant on her to provide jobs, make sales, train workers, and intervene with health services for her disabled workers. She insists on understanding and being able to perform every aspect of any job she bids on. This allows her to be knowledgeable in bidding on work as well as being able to train her employees for each job, yet she needs to delegate some authority so that MMS would not face collapse if Karin could not continue to perform every management job.

Transportation for employees is another area that needs improvement. The majority of her employees work part time rather than full time. Independent living arrangements near the company for the disabled workers would allow Karen and her employees greater flexibility.

Karin Hazam's greatest asset is her determination. She really doesn't accept "No"- she does not accept defeat - and that habit of positive thinking carries over to MMS.

Answers to Discussion Questions
by Carol P. Harvey

1. In this case was it an advantage, a disadvantage or both for Karin Hazam to be physically challenged?

Advantages can include:

- Better understanding of the situation of her employees and their needs

- Ability to offer her customers the advantage of government tax credits

- Appreciation and more realistic expectations of physically challenges workers

- Providing a role model for her employees and an example for other businesses

Disadvantages can include:

- Having to be very careful not to identify too closely with her employees situation to the detriment of good business (such as not disciplining or discharging employees who are not performing)

- Encountering discrimination against her and the company because of the high percentage of physically challenged workers

  Students may also indicate that it was both an advantage and a disadvantage and cite additional reasons. Karin herself feels that it is an advantage to be deaf because she never heard the word "no". Consequently, she felt that she could accomplish anything that she set out to do.

2. List the specific ways that Karin Hazam "manages diversity" at Mail Management Systems.

- She accepts people's differences and has treated difference as an asset not a liability

- She sees her employees in terms of their potential contribution to the business and society in general rather than as numbers, and quotas, etc.

- She offers opportunities to any employee because of what he/she can do rather than to fill a EEO quota

  Another approach to this question is to ask students to refer back to R.Roosevelt Thomas' article, From Affirmative Action to Valuing Diversity and ask them to consider how Mail Management Systems compares to Thomas' vision of the diverse organization.

3. Discuss Karin Hazam's management style in terms of planning, organizing, motivating and controlling.

Planning:
- Karin, like many entrepreneurs, does not do a great deal of long range planning. As her business grows, she will have to think more about the future.

Organizing:
- Instead of deciding what jobs need to be filled and then recruiting the appropriate workers, Karin often hires a worker and then seeks additional jobs that the person is capable of doing.

Motivating:
- Karin is charismatic in a very quiet way. Her own achievements provide a role model for her employees. She also fosters a spirit of team work by requiring that the most able employees help the less able.

Controlling:
- Karin is careful about the quality of her company's output and works to establish an atmosphere of trust where all employees carry some responsibility for the quality control function.

4. What are your major concerns for the future of this business?

In recent years the company has flourished by diversifying into providing new types of services such as recycling. With the passage of the ADA and the eventual upswing in the Massachusetts economy, this company has the potential to grow and provide many more jobs for physically and mentally challenged workers. However, the company is too dependant on Karin. She functions as the sales force, human resource manager, production scheduler, etc. As the company grows, she is going to have to develop and train employees and learn to delegate more responsibility to other workers.

The Cracker Barrel Restaurant

by John Howard

Instruction Notes

Do not allow students to write off the Cracker Barrel case as an aberration - an isolated, regionally-specific incident. Nor should they view the case solely as the work of a single, uneducated, authoritarian president. Such events occur with great frequency across North America, initiated by managers of various class and educational levels. Though intolerance of homosexuality is indeed greater in the South than elsewhere, homophobia is not limited to the region. Press students to look beyond a simplistic explanation of the case as "hicks" harassing lesbians and gays.

Student responses to the second part of question #1 should illuminate anxieties and fears that underlie employment discrimination based on sexual orientation. Therefore, do not squelch students whose remarks appear homophobic. Moreover, encourage fellow students in their attack or defense of such positions.

Build empathy for the fired Cracker Barrel employees. It may prove helpful to single-out the most virulently homophobic student and have him or her imagine being fired for appearing to be gay or lesbian. Stress how subjective such judgments can be.

Of the video pieces available on this case, the "20/20" segment is most compelling. Despite whatever regional differences may exist between students and Cracker Barrel protesters in styles of dress and speech patterns, you may elicit positive responses to Cheryl Summerville as she explains her story. Scenes of Summerville at home, playing with her dog and sitting with her lover as she knits, may help humanize the episode and allow students to overcome prejudices.

Finally, emphasize that employment discrimination against lesbians and gays remains within the law in most parts of the United States, not just in the South. Examine the cost- effectiveness of legislation on a city-by-city, county-by-county, and state-by-state basis as compared to proposed federal legislation that would protect all employees across the country. Note that the Cracker Barrel employees were never re-hired and that Cracker Barrel Old Country Store was never brought to trial.

Editor's Note: Many communities such as Aspen, Colorado and Kaizer, Oregon are passing lesbian and gay discrimination ordinances.

Answers to Discussion Questions

1. How could Cracker Barrel's initial policy statement have been "well-intentioned"? What benefits did Cracker Barrel achieve by ridding itself of lesbian and gay employees? What were the disadvantages?

> Cracker Barrel management apparently felt that their customers generally disapproved of homosexuality. Thus, their intention was to limit customer contact with lesbians and gays by firing lesbian and gay employees. Ostensibly, the company then would avoid any potential ill-will from customers preferring not to be served by lesbians or gays - especially those customers who erroneously believed that AIDS, a disease affecting a substantial portion of North America's gay male population, could be transmitted by food servers. Such reasoning falsely assumed, however, that customers could readily detect the sexual orientation of an employee. Detrimentally, the publicity surrounding the boycott insured that at least one segment of the population - activists and their supporters - would refuse to patronize Cracker Barrel. These lost customers surely outnumbered any persons who would choose Cracker Barrel solely because they discriminated. Moreover, by purging lesbians and gays, Cracker Barrel lost some of its

most talented and experienced workers. For example, Cheryl Summerville (who, as a cook, had no direct contact with customers) received excellent performance evaluations throughout her three years of service to the company. Finally, after developing a reputation as a discriminator, Cracker Barrel likely complicated its future relationships with customers and local government officials in expansion sites.

2. How should the perceived values of a customer base affect a company's personnel policies? In a large, national corporation, should personnel policies be uniform across all operating units or can they be tailored by region according to local mores?

> All well-managed companies are attentive to the needs of their customers. Employees who deal directly with patrons are expected to be courteous and efficient. Non-task-related matters such as an employee's sexual orientation, however, should remain outside the purview of the employer. Attempts to ascertain and adhere to all desires (and prejudices) of the customer ultimately lead to the impingement of the employee's dignity as an individual and rights as a worker. Though U.S. civil rights law does not yet address sexual orientation, much legislation pertaining to the workplace is federal and thereby national in scope, thus precluding regional differentiation in company policy toward personnel.

3. How well did Cracker Barrel handle its public relations efforts? After the virtual shut-down in communications with the press, how could management have re-opened discussions of the issue?

> Press accounts of the incident depicted a company that was deceitful, inflexible, and unyielding. Cracker Barrel's public relations efforts seemed to confirm that portrayal. While declaring that the company had made a full retraction, Dan Evins reiterated his misgivings about lesbian and gay employees in an interview with The Tennessean newspaper of Nashville. By then refusing any further comment on the matter, the company left itself open to the harshest criticism from national print and television media. After this point, opposition to Cracker Barrel would only be alleviated through a public acknowledgment of wrong-doing, an unequivocal statement of apology, and concrete evidence of corrective measures-at a minimum, an internal review; at most, a company-wide policy forbidding discrimination against lesbians and gays and a reinstatement of the fired workers.

4. What rights do shareholders have in the running of a publicly-held corporation?

> As part owners of a corporation, shareholders have a financial stake and thus a compelling interest in the policies and procedures of a company. A significant holding of stock, usually interpreted as 1,000 shares or more, is required of anyone wishing to put forward a resolution for a vote by the shareholders. Personnel policy resolutions typically are not viewed as "frivolous" or a matter of "ordinary business operations" if they address pressing social issues such as gender and racial discrimination. As such, they are subject to the political climate in which they are presented. After a new Democratic administration gained control in Washington in 1993, federal courts seemed willing to overturn the SEC's ruling in favor of Cracker Barrel.

5. How would you draft a new personnel policy for Cracker Barrel?

> The most comprehensive measure would be to expand the company's Equal Employment Opportunity statement to prohibit discrimination not just on the basis of race, color, sex, creed, national origin, and disability, but also on the basis of sexual orientation and HIV status.

Mobil Oil Corporation

Instruction Notes
by Eileen Hogan

Synopsis

The case describes the attempts of Mobil Oil Corporation to manage the increasing diversity of its workforce. Mobil Oil identified its need to manage the new workforce a number of years ago, and has been cited in published articles as a leader in the efforts to manage diversity. Exactly how have they done this?

The case chronicles Mobil's actions over the past five years, including management training courses, counseling programs, career planning systems, and publicity efforts. Some of these efforts were more successful than others; discussion of various participants' perceptions of these programs is offered.

The case ends with a discussion of changes in Mobil's overall management style in recent years, and its impact on the management of diversity. Mobil's current CEO has decentralized many aspects of the corporation, including planning for the management of diversity. As a result, such planning now takes place within Mobil's divisions, rather than as a corporate function. Divisions within Mobil vary widely in their own structures, systems, cultures, and leadership styles. As a result, the programs they propose to manage diversity are quite different from each other. The case describes two divisions' very different programs for managing diversity. Students are left to discuss the pro's and con's of each department's proposals, given the different ways of operating in the two divisions.

Teaching Objectives

- Introduce students to the need for managing diversity in the workplace;

- Explain how one corporation foresaw the need to manage diversity assertively and productively;

- Describe how one corporation has attempted various devices for increasing its capabilities for managing diversity;

- Explore how diversity can be managed in a decentralized corporate environment.

First, students should be made aware of the extent of and trends in diversity in the workplace, by lecture or by outside reading. Some suggestions for outside reading are given in the references.

Students should recognize that the move toward managing diversity has progressed far beyond mere affirmative action. Particularly recommended is the article by Thomas, which highlights how current perspectives on managing diversity focus on taking advantage of diversity rather then treating it as a problem. The case also discusses how Mobil attempts to do this. The article by Braham cited in the case provides some good anecdotes about how the new approach to diversity differs.

One question that might be asked of students is why Mobil, of all the oil companies, should be so proactive on this issue. Mobil executives clearly recognized this as a potential issue far before most of their peers. The answer may lie in the previous location of Mobil's headquarters in New York City, with what is obviously an extremely diverse population. This makes Mobil's move to Fairfax County more interesting - as Fairfax County is substantially less diverse than New York City. Not presented in the case is the information that the particular area in which Mobil is located within the County is mostly white middle class "yuppies"; areas of Fairfax County with the largest number of ethnic minorities are located at the Eastern edge of the county, with no easy access. Probably Mobil's extensive international experiences also contributed to their recognition of the diversity issue, as well.

The case describes Mobil's proactive approach to managing diversity. While Mobil is not typical for the oil industry, its attempts are typical of many companies in other industries. Keys to these programs are their multi-faceted nature and their head-on approach to discussing differences between people.

Managing Diversity in Economic Downturn

Mobil's challenge in managing diversity is particularly interesting because of the downturn in the economy in general and its industry in particular. How does one create a more diverse workforce which is particularly long-term and stable? The case describes Mobil's "we'll do the best that we can" approach, as well as their success.

Evidence for the loyalty of the workforce is present in the large percentage of employees who moved from New York City to Fairfax County, despite the considerable culture change and upheaval that moving causes. In return, the company appears to care about its employees and provide them with excellent benefits.

Decentralization

Mobil recently decentralized in an attempt to become more responsive to its environment. The company then faced the dilemma of how to provide a strong thrust in the area of managing diversity, while allowing components of the firm to meet goals in their own ways. The case details how this problem was managed by describing the culture of two divisions and explaining how they each came up with their own plans for managing diversity.

The Exploration and Producing Division is one of these. It currently went through substantial culture change to a more team-oriented, self-managing value system. The Marketing and Refining Division is the other; it retains Mobil's old traditional culture. Students can be asked to explore the appropriateness of each division's culture to its mission as well as the adequacy of the plans for managing diversity in each. Particular attention might be paid to the likelihood of each division's actually implementing the plans they laid out.

Future Issues

The case ends by pointing out a few issues for the future workforce that complicate this issue even further: work and family conflicts, and the educational level of the workforce. These provide an introduction for future human resource management issues.

References

——, "Workforce 2000 Today: A Bottom-Line Concern," Special report by Towers Perrin, March 1992.

——, "Workforce 2000: Gaining Competitive Advantage—Whose Job Is It?" Proceedings of the Georgetown Symposium sponsored by Georgetown University School of Business and Towers Perrin, April 1992.

——, "Workforce 2000—Competing in a Seller's Market: Is Corporate America Prepared?" Special Report by the Hudson Institute and Towers Perrin, August, 1990.

Braham, Jim, "No, You Don't Manage Everyone the Same," Industry Week, February 6, 1989, pp. 28-30, 34-35.

Solomon, Julie, "Firms Address Workers' Cultural Variety" The Differences are Celebrated, Not Suppressed," Wall Street Journal, February 10, 1989, pp. 5-6.

Thomas , R. Roosevelt, Jr., "From Affirmative Action to Affirming Diversity," Harvard Business Review, Mar/Apr 1990, 68:2, pp. 107-117.

1. Briefly contrast the approaches for managing diversity taken by the Exploring & Producing (E&P) Division and the Marketing & Refining (M&R) Division.

E & P Approach:

> A team, diverse in gender, geographic location, salary level, and minority composition, devised a plan encompassing awareness training and management training using vertical slices of company personnel.

M & R Approach:

> This division did not go through intentional cultural change. Each unit developed its own plan with the Employee Relations Manager charged with the responsibility.

What do you see as the strengths of each approach?

E & P Strengths:

- Approach gave some assurance that time and care were devoted to formalizing the plan.

- The diverse composition of the committee

- Top management approval and support obtained.

M & R Strengths:

- Freedom to custom plan to each unit's situation

- Greater opportunity for more people to participate in the plan which affects them

Which Approach do you think will result in the greatest commitment among current employees? Why?

> Student answers will vary depending on how much they value the strengths of each approach. To further explore this question, it is helpful to ask students for the potential weakness of each approach.

2. Which division do you think used the most participatory system of devising their plans for managing diversity? Why?

> Some students will say E & R because of the diversity of the planning team and because there is no way to know how participatory M & R planning actually was. Some students will say M & R because of the smaller size of the units developing the plan.

3. How do you think Mobil's plans for managing diversity will make it more competitive.

> Mobil should have lower costs due to lower turnover, lower absenteeism, and higher productivity. Since Mobil is downsizing, these personnel factors are especially important.

> Better problem-solving and greater creativity and innovation should result from having a diversity of backgrounds and perspectives.

> Mobil's diversity community outreach programs should give them a "good employer" public image, thereby giving them the pick of the best quality job seekers.

Diversity management should create flexibility in the system so that Mobil can respond faster to new opportunities.

The minorities in the sales force in the M & R division are likely to understand their ethnic markets better than outsiders and to have better credibility in those markets.

4. In some cultural groups, employees do not take the initiative nor do they talk casually with their supervisors. How might members of these groups feel in a participative management environment?

Such employees will probably be uncomfortable in a participative management environment. If they can get past their discomfort with management, they may well find the team approach very compatible with their cultural backgrounds.

SECTION IV
Exercises: *Administration Instructions*

I Am ...

by June Allard

Administration Instructions

Goals:

1. To help students learn about themselves by examining their group memberships, i.e., dimensions of culture, by which they define themselves.

2. To further examine student self-descriptors for indications of group memberships they perceive as most important.

Time Required:

30 minutes

Materials:

Student Instruction sheets from text, pens or pencils, chart pad or board, and markers

Instructions:

1. Tell the students to think about how they would describe themselves to someone they have never met and then write a single word descriptor on each of the 20 lines on their instruction sheets.

2. Stop description writing after five minutes. Tell students to draw an "X" thru any remaining blank lines. (This will discourage later additions to their lists when they listen to those given by other students.)

3. Ask students to put a star by the three most important descriptors.

4. Ask students to read aloud (or write on the board*) the descriptors they starred. Discuss similarities in dimensions and why these were felt to be the most important. Note whether most descriptors are visible dimensions such as gender and race, or are roles such as student, breadwinner, etc. Discuss differences in starred descriptors as well.

5. Ask students to read aloud (or write on the board) the first three or four descriptors they wrote. Discuss similarities in dimensions and differences and why these were the first descriptors named. Do the same with the last descriptors.

6. Discuss whether the dimensions named differed for males and females and for any other groups represented in the class. Do men write more descriptors than women? Do whites' descriptions differ from minorities' descriptions? Are descriptors such as age, social class, geographic location listed? Why or why not?

*Suggestion: Males and females can write their descriptors on separate boards or, if the class is heterogeneous, use separate boards for white/nonwhite or for dominant/nondominant ethnic groups.

What is Your Workforce I.Q.?
American or Canadian Version

by Carol P. Harvey

Administration Instructions

Goals:

1. To make the students aware of the dramatic changes that are occurring in the population.

2. To begin the discussion about how these changes impact business decisions, the management of the workforce and the need to understand diverse co-workers and consumers.

Time Required:

10-25 minutes total

- 5-10 minutes to complete the questionnaire

- Discussion time can vary from 5 to 15 minutes according to the instructor's needs

Materials:

"What Is Your Workforce I.Q.?" worksheet from text, pens/pencils, board or flip charts, and markers.

Instructions:

1. The best time to administer this exercise is at the very beginning of the course, preferably even before you review the syllabus with the class.

2. Tell the students that you are going to give them a short quiz on the workforce. Although the students will score their own quizzes, you will not collect or grade these papers.

3. Instruct the students to complete the worksheet by marking the statements as true or false and then tallying up the number of true or false statements.

4. When the class has finished, ask students to raise their hands according to the number of false answers that they have and record these totals on the board. (i.e., # who have one false answer, # who have two false answers, # who have three false answers, etc.)

5. Tell the class that all of these statements are TRUE. Most students mark 4-5 of these as false. Usually, no more than one or two students per class mark all statements as true.

6. List each of the major dimensions of diversity: age, race, ethnicity, gender, physical challenge and sexual preference on the board or on flip chart pages. Be sure to allow enough space.

7. Use these statements as a basis for beginning the discussion of the changing population in terms of the dimensions of diversity represented by the questions. Ask the students what the business implications are, i.e., challenges and opportunities, of the each of these changes and record their answers on the board.

For example, typical student responses to the increasing age of the population include: less mobility for younger workers, increased opportunities to market new products that appeal to older consumers, shifting emphasis in benefit packages from issues such as childcare to long term disability, retirement, etc.

8. Continue the discussion by asking the students what the business implications of each of the other dimensions of diversity are: race, ethnicity, gender, physical challenge and sexual preference. It is important that you record key words from student answers on the board or flip charts because the implications of these changes make a much stronger impact when it is visual.

Notice that questions # 4 and 5 are designed to call students' attention to the growth of diverse marketing opportunities and the need to understand these customers.

NOTE: If you prefer to use student groups in this exercise, step #7 can be done by assigning small groups of 4-6 students to each aspect of diversity. Then have a spokesperson present the group's findings to the whole class as in step #8.

Exploring Diversity on Your Campus

by Herbert Bromberg
and Carol Harvey

Administration Instructions

Goals:

1. To illustrate to students that diversity enriches their learning/living experience

2. To illustrate how lack of differences leads to less creativity and limited perspectives

3. To illustrate that their college experience may or may not reflect the diversity of the outside world

Time Required:

15-20 MINUTES

Materials:

Student worksheet from text, board/chart pad and markers

> This exercise is designed to be used to illustrate for relatively homogeneous student populations that their experiences in the classroom, in dorm life, and in extracurricular activities are limited in scope and experience by a lack of diversity. If your class is homogeneous in gender, race, age, or religious composition, use this exercise in the first class to illustrate why these students need to understand differences.

Instructions:

1. Ask the students to describe the _____ (your school) faculty and administration in terms of aspects of diversity, but try to let them select the order of the topics, i.e., race, gender and so forth.

   They will usually start with the most visible, i.e., % that are male/female, white/non-white, etc. You may choose to prod them to include other categories like income, age, (this will surprise you!), ethnicity, sexual orientation, religion, etc. or wait until the end of the discussion to see if these ever get raised. List all of these on the blackboard.

2. Ask the same questions about the student body. List these answers in a column next to the faculty/administration answers.

3. Ask if they see any similarities/differences between the two groups. Does this cause any problems?

4. How does this homogeneity (or heterogeneity, if you have it), among the faculty affect the learning/classroom experience?

What does a diverse faculty add to the learning experience? If students have difficulty with this question, ask if anyone who has attended another college where there was a more diverse faculty. Students may cite examples of female English professors choosing different authors, Afro-American faculty giving a contrasting perspective on the civil rights movement, Jewish faculty having a different viewpoint on the Holocaust, young faculty being easier to talk to about personal matters, etc. How might diverse administrators change the policies of the college?

5. If the student body is homogenous, how does this homogeneity affect classroom learning, dorm life, etc.? Students may cite less interesting class discussions, limited perspectives, but a higher comfort level with people who are like themselves.

]If you have one or two non-traditional students in your class, they may provide interesting observations that are quite different from those of younger students.

6. What problems does homogeneity cause? This question leads students to reflect on the fact their college population does not reflect the demographics of the world outside or prepare them for entering the workforce of the 21st century.

7. Ask them what can be done in terms of diversity to enrich their college experiences.

NOTE: They may not recognize other less visible aspects of diversity, such as sexual orientation, geographic origins, social class, income levels etc., present in the faculty, administration and the student body and this should be brought to their attention if it does not come out in the discussion. This question should lead to a discussion of AA/EEO and reverse discrimination in terms of hiring practices, admission policies, and so forth.

Increasing Multicultural Understanding: *Uncovering Stereotypes*

Administration Instructions

Goals:

1. To help individuals become aware of their own values

2. To show individuals how their culture programs them to react to and judge others in automatic and stereotypic ways

3. To discover the types and sources of stereotypes about others

4. To provide an opportunity for participant to see how their stereotypes create barriers to appreciating individual differences

Time Required:

Approximately 40 minutes to one hour.

Materials:

Uncovering Stereotypes" Student Instructions, Student Worksheet, Group Summary Sheet (all from the text) and pencils.

Instructions:

1. Instruct students to form groups with no more than 4-6 per group. Group size should be small enough to encourage active participation and maximum discussion. Chairs should be in a circular configuration where participants can face one another.

2. Instruct students to turn to "Uncovering Stereotypes" worksheet in the text. Note that the blank category boxes should be completed by either the instructor assigning categories that reflect different special populations (e.g., hillbilly, migrant worker, Jews, etc.) or by allowing the students to choose the categories that may be significant to them.

3. Instruct participants (working alone) to look at the First Thought/Judgment Column and immediately write their first thought or judgment. For example, are their first thoughts/judgments about the category immoral, greedy, hard working, ambitious, dirty, etc.?

4. Instruct students to rate each thought/judgment as positive (+), negative (-) or neutral (0) in the Rating column.

5. In the Sources column have the participants identify the source(s) of their thoughts and judgments. For example, parents, television, friends, school, etc. (Total time for steps 1, 2, 3 and 4: 15-20 minutes)

6. Instruct each group to complete the Group Summary Sheet by ventering a quick count of positive, negative and neutral thoughts/judgments for each Source Category. Students often have more negative than positive thoughts/judgments even for categories that they have no real experience with such as woman President.

---

*Adapted from Dr. John Bowman, Pembroke State University of the University of South Carolina

7. Participants in each group should reflect on the influence of their culture on their first reactions and judgments about others who are different from themselves. Use the remaining class time for a general class discussion of stereotyping in which the group shares what they have learned about the sources and judgments that influence their perceptions and actions about groups.

Then discuss the implications of having negative or positive stereotypes/judgments. For example, having a negative stereotype about working mothers taking too much time off for child care can negatively influence a manager's hiring/promotion decisions for mothers of young children.

Individuals often make stereotypic judgments about groups primarily because:

- It reduces the ambiguity about dealing with representatives of these groups.

- Negative judgments can make individuals feel superior to members of other groups.

Discuss some of the advantages and disadvantages of stereotyping, and remind the students that stereotypes are neither good nor bad, but it is what we do with those thoughts and judgments that count.

Editors' Note: It is important to be aware that an organization recently lost a discrimination lawsuit where stereotypes - raised during a training session - were introduced as evidence against the corporation. Consequently, care should be taken when using this exercise to stress that participants may be giving popular stereotypes that do not necessarily reflect their own personal views.

Invisible Volleyball Game

by Barton Kunstler

Administration Instructions

Goals:

This activity is designed to help students understand that:

1. Males and females in our society may experience sports differently from one another

2. Sports experience tends to reinforce and exaggerate gender-associated differences in managerial behaviors, attitudes, and values

3. Managerial culture often self-selects for advancement those people conversant with the values and vocabulary of sports culture

4. Understanding the ever changing role of sports in our society, especially in regard to gender-related values and behaviors, is a potent source of societal and organizational reform

Time Required:

This exercise, including discussion, takes about 1 hour, 20 minutes of class time. If the role play is used, it can take 2 1/2 hours. Instructors can compress the discussion to fit the activity into a 1 hour class, if necessary.

Materials:

Student Observation Sheets from the text, a small open area, board or flip chart, and imagination.

Instructions:

The following set of instructions contains directions the teacher gives to the class as well as notes from the author to the teacher that will help the activity run smoothly. The entries are numbered in the sequence they occur during the exercise, and the directions to the class are clearly labeled with the phrases, "Ask/Tell the class".

1. Preliminary observations:

   a. Some open space is needed for the game, either at the front or back of the room, or in the center of a horseshoe arrangement.

   b. As few as four members of one sex is enough for a game.

   c. The instructor should refrain from playing, as his/her behavior may influence the groups' responses.

   d. If students ask you to justify using an invisible ball (instead of a balloon, ball, or rolled-up sock), explain that an imaginary ball is more practical for the space and that an invisible ball equalizes skill levels.

   e. Keep directions at a minimum, as described below.

2. Tell the class:

> We are going to play a volleyball game — two games, actually. The women will play one game among themselves, as will the men. We will use an invisible ball and invisible net. As each group plays, the other will observe and take notes. Will either group volunteer to go first? If not, let's flip a coin.

3. Tell the class:

> Now that we know who is going first, organize a game and start playing. Members of the other group, observe and keep notes on your observation sheets.
> Approximate time for explanations: 5 minutes

4. Note:

> Because the significant activity begins as soon as the first group begins to organize its game, do not suggest how to choose teams, define the court, or conduct play. Instructions to the observing group should be kept similarly minimal, in order to avoid indicating to players what is expected of them. Offer observers only the directions found on their "Observation Sheet".

5. Duration of Game:

> The first group of students play, usually till about 6-10 points are scored (for example, 5-4, 3-3), or 5-7 minutes go by. Then the groups switch roles and the second game is played.
> Approximate time: 15 minutes (20 minutes running total).

> NOTE: Often, students will express self-consciousness via giggling, hesitancy about playing, etc. Be encouraging without discussing the game itself. The self-consciousness felt by people is a part of the activity and is relevant to the discussion.

6. Writing Down Student Responses:

> Divide the board or flip chart in half, labelling one area "Women" and the other "Men". Write down the terms the students use to describe the two groups' styles.

7. Ask the class:

> How did the two groups differ in how they approached, organized, and played the game? Start by describing your observations of the other group, but interject your perceptions about your own group as well. Compare such aspects as playing style, teamwork, and organization of the game.

Suggested Questions:

Instructor, pose leading questions to stimulate ideas. Some examples:

- Was there a difference in how the two groups chose up sides?

- Which group was more competitive?

- You say the women talked with each other more than the men did. Does this imply the women were more teamwork-oriented?

- If the men passed the ball more, does that imply that they were more team-oriented?

- How do your observations relate to the readings?

Frequently raised issues:

> Almost always you will get 10-20 entries for both the men's and the women's side, and the level of observation and detail may be surprising. Some issues that always arise include: how the two groups organized the game; the role of non-game related behaviors; which group was more concerned with the score; which side had more fun; and the relative prevalence of game playing behaviors, such as spiking and passing. Approximate time of discussion: 20 minutes (40 minutes running total)

8. Tell the class:

> Imagine now that each of these two lists represents a profile of someone up for a management job. The person can be male or female. You are the committee deciding this person's future. I (the instructor) will play devil's advocate for either side you argue. But let's start off with why the person on the women's list would not make a good manager. After a few such reasons, you can start defending this person so that we'll get a debate going on the pros and cons of each of the two profiles.

> Now do the same with the person represented by the men's list. Approximate time: 15 minutes (55 minutes running total).

9. Ask the class:

How does this argument reflect:

> a. How managers are viewed and evaluated in the workplace?

> b. How these traits and our attitudes towards them reflect current trends and theories in managerial style, behavior, and function?

> c. How does this discussion reflect the actual experiences you have had in the workplace, in terms of how people are perceived, how they are promoted, and attitudes towards men and women and the behaviors considered appropriate to each?
> Approximate time: 10 minutes (65 minutes running total).

10. Instructor, start off with the women's list because it contains more non-traditional managerial attributes, and thus the class will tend to voice more typical perceptions first. When the class criticizes the person with the male associated attributes, it will tend to challenge accepted stereotypes of proper managerial behavior, and also the behavior we unconsciously expect from men and women.

Instructor, use your role as devil's advocate to challenge any position, for example: "What if this person is a guy? Sure, it's okay for a woman to be like this, but we can't hire a wimpy male." Pursue ideas: "Is this an underlying attitude towards women as well, that they're not tough enough? What happens when they act tough? What attitudes are directed towards them?" "Do we really want this aggressive, rigid guy barging in here with his macho attitudes? What is it like to work for someone like this?"

Optional Role Play

The class breaks into groups of at least four people and develops a role play using the following roles: a male acting according to the male team's profile as described by the class; a female acting according to the female team's profile; a male acting out the female profile; and a female acting out the male profile. If the class is not evenly divided by sex, variations can be developed, and if groups need to be larger than 4 people, roles can be duplicated. Each group practices and then performs the role play, which can be about 5 minutes long. After the role play, each group relates the points it intended to demonstrate, and class discussion ensues. Approximate time: 1 1/4 hour with four groups.

---

11. Ask the class:

In what ways do girls' and boys' experiences with sports contribute to the pattern that emerged in our volleyball game? What do you remember growing up, or observe in kids today, that is similar to or different from what you observed in our game? Approximate time: 15 minutes (1 hour, 20 minutes running total).

NOTE: Discussion usually revolves around team building and group behavior, the role of coaches and mentors in life and at work, social skills developed on court, and competitiveness. One recurring theme has been that, on the one hand, sports supposedly teaches teamwork, a lesson from which men benefit. On the other, women are often seen as more relationship oriented. How can we resolve this apparent paradox? What are the cultural equivalents of sports that teach young girls lessons in teamwork and group relationships? What are the negative contributions of sports to team and group behavior? Will women benefit from the upsurge in female students' sports programs initiated since Title IX? Both men and women do note differences in how the two sexes respond to teamwork, competition, and coaching roles at work, and the connection to sports is a rich way to analyze professional roles.

A related area is the impact of sports on managerial/professional culture. This goes beyond people's ability to "play the game" at work, which tends to be the focus in the literature. The issue speaks to the role of sports and/or team experience in defining work culture itself. Does sports help create a system that, in turn, self-selects people whose values are those of the dominant sports culture, thus affecting careers and organizational culture? Or do sports and organizational cultures both stem from some more primary cultural matrix?

Additional Observations:

The results of this activity have been, in our experience, fairly consistent. Men choose up sides and set up the game in a more formal, rule oriented way; they are more aggressive in their play; and they tend to be more concerned about the score, more likely to spike and pass, and more focused on the game itself. Women seem to have more fun; talk more during the game; act more relaxed; and spike, pass, keep score, and rotate positions less. The women tend to choose up sides more casually, and are less likely to engage in pep talk.

Sometimes, students challenge the methodology of the activity; for instance, the group that goes first being more self-conscious, etc. There is some validity to this argument, but the contrast between the two groups will usually be sufficiently pronounced to allow the instructor to respond that the order of who goes first is not responsible for the differences. The instructor can also refer to the history of the activity, which shows that the order has some, but not a great deal of influence on behavior.

If the men play first, the women are more likely to play hard, having seen the game modelled; in effect, the ice is broken. But in all cases, the pattern has held, even when 1 or 2 women have tried to generate a more intensive game. This held true even when one women's group included several members of a college volleyball team!

This pattern is almost too good to be true from an instructor's point of view; it is perhaps discouraging from a societal perspective. Interesting points do emerge in relation to this almost stereotypical division:

A. Management is changing in all professions. Qualities traditionally viewed as being more female in nature, such as decentralization, consensus-building, and emphasis on process and communication, are becoming more valued, although perhaps not as widely as the literature and training seminars might lead one to think. The experiences students bring from their own workplaces are immensely informative in evaluating current attitudes towards the sexes and towards various management styles, and serve as an important stimulus to discussion.

B. The greater participation of females in sports over the past 15 years has created a convergence in terms of women's and men's behaviors and attitudes. In addition, a mix of so-called male and female qualities are increasingly viewed as vital for a successful manager. Nonetheless, every group notes the continued existence of stereotypes about work styles, and the durability of the glass ceiling and implicit sexist attitudes at work.

C. Some participants point out that in their actual sports experience, women do play more aggressively than they did in the invisible volleyball game. Yet, others note cases where co-ed games evolved or devolved into all-male games, or ended up dominated by one or two aggressive men. Discussion of this behavior, and various levels of complicity (even unwilling or unconscious), can be extremely lively and interesting. Also, the instructor can point out that the fact that the activity brought out a certain type of behavior, may be a noteworthy indicator in itself.

D. The role of childhood sports in helping people learn to negotiate differences, gain entry into groups, understand the roles they must play in groups, etc., is a major area of concern in these discussions. As such, sports itself becomes a metaphor for all the ways boys and girls are conditioned in our society, and the impact of this conditioning on career choices and success.

Physically Challenged Students:

Because the ball is invisible, anyone who has the physical ability to come to class can participate in the exercise. Wheelchair athletes in particular are accomplished in many sports and can certainly play in this game, and may provide interesting views both from the sports and the job-related perspectives.

Video:

This exercise would seem to be made for video, but it works very well without it, and simple observation yields a rich harvest of perceptions.

Conclusion:

This exercise is fun, embraces a wide variety of themes, is adaptable for many types of groups, and energizes the classroom. It reveals a great deal about gender expectations in the workplace and on the playing field, and about the role of sports in defining gender in our society.

Selected Reading List

The following texts provide useful preparation for the issues raised by this exercise:

Out of the Bleachers, edited by Stephanie Twin, with an excellent introduction by Twin and relevant selections by such writers as Ann Crittendon, Olga Connolly, Jack Scott, and Harry Edwards. The Feminist Press, CUNY, NY, 1979.

The Managerial Woman by Margaret Hennig and Anne Jardim. A landmark study with important passages on teamwork and upbringing. Pocket Books, NY, 1976, 1977.

The Male Machine by Marc Feigen Fasteau. An extended essay on male attitudes at work and play, and their interrelationships. Dell Publishing Co., NY, 1975.

Are We Winning Yet? by Mariah Burton Nelson. Valuable essays on the current roles and role models in women's sports today.

Challenging the Men: Women in Sport by K.F. Dyer. Contains a great deal of technical information on women's physical capabilities, conditioning, and gender issues and their relationship to research about female and male physical capabilities.

History of Sport and Physical Activity in the United States by Betty Spears and Richard Swanson. An interesting historical survey that considers issues of gender, class, race, and multicultural perspectives. William C. Brown, 2nd edition.

Surfacing Student Sexism and Raising Consciousness through the Use of an Opinion Questionnaire

by Gerald D. Klein

Administration Instructions

Goals:

1. To foster discussion about the changing roles of men and women

2. To examine the extent to which students hold traditional sex role stereotypes

3. To focus students on stereotypical attitudes about women and work

Time Required:

45-60 minutes

Materials:

Women and Work opinion questionnaire from the text, optional summary sheets, pencils, board or chart pad and markers.

Instructions:

To many teaching in the organizational behavior area, the desirability and need for addressing the changing roles of women and men and traditional sex role stereotypes are well established. But how can this be done in a way that is both effective, in the sense of stimulating student reflection and producing desirable changes in perceptions and attitudes, and time-efficient? Lecturing and exhortation on these issues are time-efficient but are not necessarily effective in modifying attitudes and behavior.

I have tried various methods to explore these issues in the classroom. One method I have tried, several varieties of which seem to be in widespread use, involves dividing the class by sex (i.e., males and females work in separate groups) and having each group compile a list of male/female similarities and a list of male/female differences. Eventually, the groups are brought together to share their lists. My experience in using this method leads me to suspect that, while most males eventually (if sometimes begrudgingly) agree that there are more similarities than differences between males and females, ingrained sexist attitudes - especially in regard to women and work - continue to persist.

More recently, I have developed and have used with more success an Opinion Questionnaire. The questionnaire is specifically designed to air for the purpose of critical examination, sexist attitudes, and stances held by students that are relevant to organizational life. The questionnaire is basically a compendium of statements that are reflective of either the position of someone who is sexist or the position of someone who is more knowledgeable, accepting, and supportive of women and the women's liberation movement. The statements that comprise the questionnaire express attitudes and beliefs about the proper social role of women, how women experience the traditional roles of house-

---

*Reprinted with permission from Gerald D. Klein and Kathryn B. Klein, Rider College, Lawrenceville, New Jersey 08648

wife and mother, the extent to which women are committed to careers, the suitability of women for managerial and leadership roles, and the women's liberation movement. Generally, students express their agreement or disagreement with these statements. From scanning the items that make up the questionnaire, it is evident that agreement with items expressing the sexist position and/or rejecting the items that represent a more enlightened position could seriously impair one's performance in most American organizations today.

Some of the items on the questionnaire appear so blatantly sexist that the reader may well wonder who would agree or, much worse, "strongly agree" with them. Repeated use in the classroom has demonstrated to the author that in most classes there will be women as well as men who will agree, if not strongly agree, with at least some of the items expressing the sexist view. In sections where relatively few students express any agreement at all with these statements, but instead seem genuinely accepting and supportive of women, I get students to frame effective rebuttals to sexist attitudes in anticipation of encountering them in the outside world.[1]

The Opinion Questionnaire as I have used it is typically distributed to students at the beginning of a class period, following a brief overview of the class session. The importance of honesty and candor in completing the instrument is stressed. Students, as they work on the questionnaire, are also encouraged to note on a separate piece of paper or in the margins of the questionnaire any elaborations or modifications of their answers that they feel compelled to make. These notes are frequently useful in the small group discussion that follows the completion of the instrument.[2]

When students have completed the questionnaire, they form groups of at least four - preferably with equal numbers of men and women - for the purpose of sharing answers. Groups are encouraged to seek or probe for the reasons for member answers, or the "data" on which answers are based. Self-disclosure, mutual confrontation, and exchange are encouraged. I have asked that students share and discuss their answers one item at a time; another approach might be to let each person present all of her of his answers at one time while the other group members record them on a separate sheet of paper or in columns added to the questionnaire itself. This strategy would largely eliminate the problem of groups running out of time and not learning where members stand on each of the items.

I have found it useful to collect and summarize class responses to the questionnaire and to make this summary available to students. The summary typically shows separately the responses of males and females. Alternatively, groups can be asked to appoint a "recorder." During the small group discussions, the recorder keeps track of the number of "strongly agrees," "agrees," etc., for each item and either provides this data to the instructor so that he or she may put it on the board or puts the data on the board himself/herself. The obvious benefit of this approach) and the approaches described below) is that comparison data are available when students are liable to have the most interest in it.

Students can also "score" their questionnaire. A scoring system allows students to compare their responses more readily with the class's, or with any other group for which similar data exist. (Although I have not yet done this myself, I would think that having questionnaire response data from various groups - e.g., male managers, members of a women's center or collective - could be very illuminating and very productive in terms of class discussion.)

---

[1]An Instructor who undertakes this exercise should be well aware of effective rebuttals to the sexist statements on the questionnaire. An instructor not sufficiently well versed on these issues can team teach this session with someone who is, at least the first few times.

[2]In lieu of using the Opinion Questionnaire itself, the instructor can have students write out answers to a series of questions drawn from the items on the questionnaire-e.g., Is it important that the husband make the larger salary if both husband and wife work? (Would you want this in your marriage?) Do you believe that women are capable of leading work groups or teams in organizations? What are your feelings about women attempting to obtain jobs usually performed by men? Would you rather work for a man or a woman? (Why?) Do you believe that in a period of high unemployment, a male applicant for a job should be given preference over a female applicant?

Scoring the questionnaire can be accomplished by assigning a numerical value (+4, +3, +2, +1) to each answer on the continuum from "Strongly agree" to "Strongly disagree" (reversing the scoring order for items 5, 8, 12, and 15), and then having students compute their total scores.

Minimum score possible is 15; maximum score possible is 60; lower scores indicate more enlightened and less sexist attitudes towards women and work. Higher scores indicate less enlightened and more sexist attitudes towards women and work.

Following about 45 minutes of small group discussion, the groups are called together for wrap-up. Identifying those items for each group and/or the class as a whole on which there was most agreement and most disagreement is a useful summarizing device. Exploring the areas where there is disagreement can focus student attention on the faulty and potentially harmful assumptions that are made about women.

If the class is well divided into sexist and antisexist camps and if sufficient energy exists, the instructor may want to spontaneously organize a formal debate on any or all of the items on the questionnaire. In this instance, the class would be broken into two or more groups, spokespersons appointed within each group, group positions worked out, etc. Alternatively, during the wrap-up part of the exercise, the instructor can ask the class for help in framing rebuttals to the sexist opinions on the questionnaire, or the instructor may offer rebuttals of his/her own. I have also asked students to share with the class, situations in which they have experienced sex-based discrimination and the ways in which they might be sexist. I have found that a good way to get discussion going here is for the instructor to share how he/she may be (or was) sexist.

The instructor may choose to amplify the discussion for some of the following topics: the phenomena of stereotyping and its effects; the pygmalion effect; what is really known about male/female differences; the processes and effects of sex-role socialization; what it means to be open rather than closed to others; equal opportunity legislation and litigation; affirmative action programs; and, assuming everything has a "cost," the costs as well as the benefits for both men and women of changing sex roles, being liberated, egalitarian marriages, and so on.

Is This Sexual Harassment?

by Carol P. Harvey

Administration Instructions

Goals:

1. To foster understanding of what constitutes sexual harassment in the workplace

2. To give students an opportunity to apply the statutes on sexual harassment to common workplace situations

Time Required:

If students are assigned the reading and completion of this exercise prior to class, the discussion takes anywhere from 20-45 minutes depending on the degree of controversy in the class.

Materials:

Each student should complete the "Is This Sexual Harassment?" worksheet from the text PRIOR to coming to class.

Instructions:

1. Assign students to read and complete the "Is This Sexual Harassment Worksheet" before coming to class.

2. Once students have decided if the ten incidents on the worksheet constitute sexual harassment, review with them the elements of sexual harassment as defined by Title VII of the Civil Rights Act of 1964 and outlined in the introductory paragraph of the exercise.

3. Go through each of the ten incidents with the class. For each one begin by asking for a show of hands for the question: "Please raise your hand if you think that this incident is sexual harassment under the law." Then ask, Please raise your hand, if you do not think that this is sexual harassment." If there is substantial disagreement, it is useful to record the "yes" and "no" votes on the board.

4. Discuss the incidents where the students either had substantial disagreement or a large percentage gave the incorrect answer.

5. Watch for "male" or "female" votes, where a large percentage of the women disagree with the men. These present good opportunities for discussion.

6. If the following points have not come out during the discussion, it may be useful to point out some of the following data:

> LEGISLATION: Under the Civil Rights Act of 1991, sexual harassment claims can include both compensatory damages for medical treatment or for pain/suffering and punitive damages for intentional discrimination. The later depends upon the number of employees in the workplace where the harassing activity took place. Companies that have 15-100 employees are limited in punitive damages to a maximum of $50,000. Larger companies with over 500 employees can pay up to #300,000.[1]

> COSTS: A survey by a magazine estimated that the costs of sexual harassment at the companies the publication surveyed were $6,719,593 per company, per year. The figure is so high because it goes beyond legal costs and includes the "costs" of lowered morale, decreased productivity, leaves of absence and employee turnover.[2]

Answers to the Incidents

1. While this is not sexual harassment, per se, it is probably an unconscious gesture that the supervisor should be more careful about. It could easily be interpreted as something more. If it makes Gary uncomfortable, he should say so.

2. Because going into the plant is part of Julie's job and the behavior of the workers has created a hostile environment, as evidenced by her being so upset, this is sexual harassment. Management needs to stop the behavior of the plant workers.

3. Because there is no evidence that this relationship is unwelcome by either party, this does not constitute sexual harassment.

4. Again, both parties seem to be willing to enter into this relationship, so it is not sexual harassment. However, if this relationship should terminate, Tom may find himself, as Jeanne's boss, in a very awkward position.

5. This appears to be a budding case of sexual harassment, because it is clearly behavior of a sexual nature. Steve is not welcoming the overture and it involves a condition of employment, a performance appraisal that will in all likelihood involve a raise and/or future promotional opportunities. However, the case does not specify if Steve has received poor performance appraisals in the past or if there have indeed been documented incidents of his not being a team player. It is very difficult for a manager to discipline a subordinate, if she/he has harassed the employee. This manager may have placed her company in a very difficult legal position.

6. This is not sexual harassment but may represent his attempt to comfort a distraught employee.

7. This is not harassment because there is no indication that the compliment is unwelcome and or that it is of a sexual nature.

8. This is not harassment. Travel is part of the job and the employee is being told this upon hiring. Many men and women travel on overnight business. From the information provided, there is no indication that any sexual favors are expected on these trips.

9. This is a classic case of sexual harassment. The unwelcome behavior of a sexual nature has repeatedly been brought to the attention of management and nothing has been done to correct Joe's behavior. Clearly, the women regard his remarks as hostile because they have taken the trouble to complain. The company's defense, "Don't be so sensitive, he doesn't mean anything by it," is not legally defensible in this case.

10. This is not sexual harassment because there is no indication that Jennifer is uncomfortable with the staring. Some people do wear revealing clothing to work to get attention. However, her supervisor should bring the issue of her inappropriate business attire to her attention before there is a problem.

Notes

[1] Norman Fritz, "Sexual Harassment and the Working Woman," Personnel (February, 1989), pp. 4-8.

[2] Timothy Noah and Albert R. Karr, "What New Civil Rights Law Will Mean," Wall Street Journal, November 4, 1991, pp. B1, B10.

Additional References

McCann, Nancy Dodd and McGinn, Thomas A. (1992). Harassed: 100 Women Define Appropriate Behavior in the Workplace. Business One Irwin: Homewood Illinois.

Wagner, Ellen J. (1992). Sexual Harassment in the Workplace. Amacon: New York.

Cultural-Diversity Quiz: How's Your "Cultural I.Q."?

Administration Instructions

Goals:

1. To demonstrate how much (or how little) students know about other cultures

2. To sensitize students to communication differences

Time Required:

50 - 45 MINUTES (10 minutes to complete questionnaire; 5 to score; discussion can vary from 15-30 minutes)

Materials:

Cultural diversity quiz: "How's Your Cultural I.Q.?" sheet from the text, pens/pencils, overheads or handouts or scoring key and evaluation of student's scores from the teacher's manual.

Instructions:

1. Instruct the students to complete the Cultural I.Q. test independently.

2. Instruct the students to score the quiz. The scoring key can be presented as an overhead.

3. Students give themselves one point for each correct answer.

4. Minimum score is 0; maximum score is 20. Interpret scores by either making an overhead or handout from the evaluation sheet.

5. Discuss student's scores as a class.

---

*Reprinted with the permission of Lexington Books, an imprint of Macmillan, Inc., from PROFITING IN AMERICA'S MULTICULTURAL WORKPLACE: How to do Business Across Cultural Lines by Sondra B. Thiederman, Ph.D. Copyright 1991 by Sondra Thiederman.

Cultural-Diversity Quiz: How's Your "Cultural I.Q."?

Answer Key

1.	a	11.	a
2.	False	12.	a, b, and c
3.	a	13.	True
4.	False	14.	a, c, and d
5.	b	15.	False
6.	False	16.	b
7.	a	17.	c
8.	d	18.	False
9.	False	19.	c
10.	c	20.	c

Evaluation Sheet
Number Correct Evaluation

16-20   Congratulations! You are a "cultural-diversity genius" and are no doubt doing very well in the multicultural business world.

11-15   You are culturally aware and are probably very receptive to learning more about cultural differences.

6-10   Oops! You have a ways to go, but are obviously interested in the subject and see the need to learn more. That's an important first step.

0-5   Do not be discouraged. The knowledge reflected in this quiz is new to most professionals in the United States.

Test of Management Knowledge in the Traditional Navajo American Indian Culture

by Fairlee E. Winfield

Administration Instructions

Goals:

1. To introduce students to a major United States Indian (Navajo) culture

2. To sensitize students to the symbols, rituals, behaviors, and beliefs of the Navajo culture

Materials:

Navajo Management Test from the text, pens/pencils and answer key for Navajo Management test from teachers manual. An overhead or handout can be made from the answer key.

Time Required:

15-30 minutes.

A "Test of Management Knowledge in the Traditional Native American Indian Culture" is contained in Chapter V of the textbook. Information to correctly answer these test questions is deliberately omitted from the Note and the Case. This has been done to intentionally increase the students' level of discomfort and thereby simulate the uneasiness associated with xenophobic responses and ethnocentricity. Students generally complain, experience anxiety, and believe the test is unfair. Therefore, adequate time should be allowed after administration of the test for venting of emotional responses. The test activity is designed to increase students' sensitivity to cultural diversity and to cross-cultural management dilemmas.

Instructions:

1. Administer the "Test of Management Knowledge in the Traditional Native American Indian Culture." Allow only about 15 minutes.

2. Score the test. (Students will do poorly.)

3. Discuss students' feelings while they were answering the questions. Were students angry? Happy? Confused? Frustrated? What was easy about the test? What was difficult? Was the test fair? Were any of these responses based on xenophobia or ethnocentrism?

4. Discuss management of culturally diverse people from the standpoint of the non-dominant group.

5. Seek opinions and responses from students with other than European American backgrounds.

1.	c	14.	b or c
2.	c	15.	c
3.	c	16.	c
4.	d	17.	b
5.	a	18.	d
6.	a	19.	d (4 is a sacred & magical number)
7.	b		
8.	c	20.	b
9.	a	21.	d
10.	a	22.	b and d
11.	b	23.	b
12.	c	24.	c
13.	c	25.	a

Creating Your Own Culture

by Art Shriberg

Administration Instructions

Goals:

1. To help students identify some of the elements of culture

2. To simulate the stress and confusion of cross-cultural business contacts

3. To develop an appreciation of diverse cultural behavior and its impact on business transactions

Time Required:

1 - 2 1/2 hours

Materials:

Student instructions and worksheets from the text, copies of facilitator's worksheet from the teacher's manual

Instructions:

This exercise can be used in any class or group from 14 - 60 members. It is especially effective with classes or workgroups that have a prior history together.

It is useful to have completed a discussion of cultural relativism, the elements of culture or aspects of diversity before presenting this exercise.

Two private spaces are needed. If necessary, one group can use a hallway; adjoining classrooms are preferable, or at least use opposite ends of a classroom.

Two students should be chosen as "cultural guides." They will lead the subgroup discussion. They should be extroverted, creative, strong students with leadership ability.

How to Proceed

The group should be introduced to the various elements of culture and different value orientations through lectures, videos, discussions, etc. It is also useful to highlight some demographic realities so that the group will realize that the "American" culture represents a small piece of the world and that there is great diversity within the United States.

1. The class should be divided into two subgroups. It is useful to have each subgroup as heterogeneous as possible. Each subgroup will be given from 30 minutes to one hour to create its own culture. Each culture will have norms concerning:

> The most respected types of people
> How respect is shown to these people
> What the culture values
> The name of the culture
> Appropriate topics of discussion in the culture
> How people behave at social events

How business is conducted
What products they sell
How the culture treats strangers and/or deviates
How people greet each other
How the culture uses non-verbal behavior
Other issues

The guide for each group will guide the group through Step 1 and then each group will practice living as members of their culture. The instructor can float and assist as necessary.

2. After the cultures are formed, each group will send representatives to the other cultures. These visitors will attempt to make a sale to the leader of the culture they are visiting.

3. The groups will then reunite for a debriefing. Each group will describe the other cultures and then their own. A general discussion will follow, if there is time.

Detailed Instructions for Instructors

1. After the initial directions are given, the group should be divided into two or more subgroups (not smaller than 8 people nor larger than 20). Distribute people among the groups to ensure as much diversity of gender, age, race, etc. as possible.

Each subgroup needs a "guide" and a "scribe" needs to be appointed to write down the culture's rules. Each student can be asked to use their worksheet. These rules should not be shown to people from other cultures. Using the student worksheet from the text, the facilitator(s) should guide the group through the process of creating its own rules. The items in parenthesis are suggestions that the facilitator might use to help the group develop its rules. These directions are for the facilitators only - do not show them to the group.

After the group defines its culture, they are instructed to live it. Ask them to walk out of the room and then re-enter "in culture;" that is, role playing according to the rules of their culture. They will feel strange at first, but they will catch on. They may need to create new rules when they are not sure how to behave (a missing cultural element). Most groups greatly enjoy this process, once they get going.

Next, choose an emissary and decide what you want to sell to the other cultures. Choose someone who is outgoing and articulate.

Note: It is useful and fun to take a coffee (or lunch) break at some point in the exercise. People need to "stay in culture" and behave according to their cultural rules during the break.

2. At a pre-arranged time, send one representative from each culture to the other culture(s) for five minutes. Make sure each group stays in culture. Have your representative debrief the group, describing the other cultures and how they conduct business. Have the scribe take private notes. Send two groups (or three or four) of emissaries two (or three) times, repeating the process.

3. When the last emissary returns, have them describe the other culture(s), using the initial categories from the student worksheets.

4. Bring the complete group together and have members of each culture describe their culture and its approach to business. (When they finish, each culture can describe itself.) Finally, the facilitator can compare the cultures created with a US culture or some others and discuss the elements of cultures.

Note: The role playing portion of this exercise can be videotaped for class discussion.

Dr Shriberg spent twenty years as a Dean or Vice President at four different universities. He has a B.S. from Wharton School, an M.A. from Boston University, an Executive MBA from Xavier University, and an Ed.D. from Columbia University. Dr. Shriberg teaches leadership and cross-cultural behavior and also consults widely for a number of international firms.

Creating Your Own Culture

Facilitator's Copy of Student Worksheet

In this exercise each group will create their own culture. There are no rights and wrongs; your culture can have any rules that the group decides, but the group is expected to follow the rules it creates throughout the exercise.

Choose one student to be the scribe and to write down your rules. For each of the following questions you might have several answers.

1. In your culture, who are the most respected people (females, males, light skin, dark skin, tall, short, bald, very hairy, other)?

2. How is this respect shown (bowing, avoiding eye contact, constant eye contact, never speaking to the person unless spoken to, other)?

3. What are the favorite topics of conversation (politics, religion, only about grandparents, only about children, other)?

4. What happens at social events (people dance only with their own gender, people are always in groups of at least four, men do most of the talking, other)?

5. How is business conducted (you get right to the point, never in front of women, only after eating, other)?

6. What will your culture sell? (Choose one product that is consistent with your cultural values.) At what price?

7. How does your culture treat strangers (very friendly, very unfriendly, only friendly to women, no eye contact, other)?

8. What does your culture value (religion, the earth, truth, productivity, relationship, beauty)? (There should be several answers to this question.)

9. How does your culture deal with people who don't know or don't follow its rules?

10. How does your culture use non-verbal behavior? What are some of your non-verbal cues?

11. What other unique elements does your culture have?

12. What is the name of your culture?

Musical Chairs

by M. June Allard

Administration Instructions

Goal:

To demonstrate the frustration of being physically challenged, i.e., unable to communicate with people in the traditional way. Note. This exercise can also be used to illustrate the difficulties and frustration encountered by those for whom English is a second language.

Time Required:

Approximately 15 to 20 minutes

Materials:

Student instructions and student worksheet from the text, pen or pencil, chart pad or board and markers or overhead projector, handouts of the solution sheet from teacher's manual or an overhead of the solution.

Instructions:

1. Instruct students to form groups of four to six members with each group sitting in a circle facing each other.

2. Ask students to read the Musical Chairs passage.

3. Each group is to solve the problem using ONLY ONE student worksheet and is to come up with ONE GROUP answer. TO SIMULATE THE FEELING OF LOSING THE CAPACITY TO SPEAK OR THE FRUSTRATION OF USING A SECOND LANGUAGE, STUDENTS ARE TOLD NOT TO COMMUNICATE VERBALLY.

> STUDENTS SHOULD BE TOLD NOT TO SOLVE THE PROBLEM INDEPENDENTLY, BUT AS A GROUP. IT MAY BE NECESSARY TO REMIND THEM OF THIS PERIODICALLY; THE INTENT IS TO FORCE THEM TO COMMUNICATE NONVERBALLY WITH EACH OTHER.

4. When the group has agreed upon an answer, one member is to raise his/her hand and share the answer on the Worksheet with the Instructor who does not speak, but signals by shaking his/her head whether or not the answer is correct.

5. Call time when about half the groups have the correct answer.

6. The solution to the problem (see solution sheet) can be written on the board or presented as an overhead or as a handout.

7. Center class discussion on how students felt while doing the exercise. Generally, students express frustration, feelings of inadequacy, irritation and even anger.

> Feedback from students for whom English is a second language indicates that they are more comfortable with this exercise than with many others because it forces native English speakers to experience what it feels like to be frustrated in trying to communicate in a less familiar way.

MUSICAL CHAIRS SOLUTION

SOLUTION STEPS	----CHAIRS----		Total	---- STUDENTS ----		Total
	RH	LH		?	?	
1. before class }	30 RH	5 LH	35			50
2. during class }				-15 RH / 20 RH	5 LH	35
3. after class }	-6 / 24 RH	-1 / 4 LH	-7 / 28			
4. later				+8 RH / 38 RH	5 LH	43
5. Total Chairs Needed	38 RH	5 LH				
Chairs in Classroom	-24 RH	-4 LH				
Chairs still Needed	14 RH	1 LH				

The Older Worker

by Stella M. Nkomo
Myron D. Fottler
and R. Bruce McAfee

Administration Instructions

Goals:

1. To familiarize students with typical stereotypes toward older workers and the managerial implications of those stereotypes

2. To provide students with factual information regarding older workers

Time Required:

15 minutes to complete the Older Worker Questionnaire.

45 minutes for group and class discussion of all items on the Older Worker Questionnaire.

Materials:

The Older Worker Student Instructions and Questionnaire from student text and solution form Teacher's Manual.

Instructions:

1. Prior to the class meeting in which this exercise will be discussed, instruct students to complete The Older Worker Questionnaire in their text.

2. At the start of the exercise, divide the class into groups of three to five students. Each group is to discuss each item on the questionnaire and arrive at a consensus regarding the correct answer (Limit students to 20 minutes).

3. After the groups have finished, present the correct answers along with an explanation (See solutions which follow).

4. Each group should record the correct answer next to their groups' answers and then compare the two to determine the number right and wrong.

---

*Reprinted with Permission from Applications in Human Resource Management, 2nd ed., by Stella M. Nkomo, Myron D. Fottler & R. Bruce McAfee. PWS. Kent, 1992

Solutions

1. False. Studies have shown that as a general rule, older employees are typically more satisfied than are younger ones. Reference: C. Tausky, Work Organizations, Peacock Publishers, 1978.

2. False. Studies across a wide range of occupations show that creative behavior peaks in the thirties or early forties, perhaps because of declining motivation to be creative later in life. Reference: H.C. Lehman, Age and Achievement, Princeton University Press, 1953.

3. True. There has been a dramatic increase in life expectancy over the past 50 years, primarily as a result of a reduction in mortality rates at younger ages. In 1940, a child could expect to live until age 63 whereas by 1980 this figure reached 74. The trend is expected to continue so that by the year 2025, the life expectancy of a 65 year old will be 83 for men and 87 for women. Reference: S.H. Sandell, Prospects for Older Workers: The Demographic and Economic Context. In, The Problem Isn't Age: Work and Older Americans, Praeger, 1987.

4. False. The proportion of persons 65 and over, which has risen from 8 percent in 1950 to 11 percent in 1980, will rise to about 13 percent in 2010 and about 20 percent in 2030. Reference: National Commission for Employment Policy, Older Workers: Prospects, Problems and Policies, U.S. Government Printing Office, 1985.

5. False. Retirement in its present form is a relatively recent development. In 1948, the labor force participation of men 65 and over was almost 50 percent, in contrast to the 16 percent rate in 1986. Further, 55 percent of men age 60-64 in 1986 were in the labor force compared to 64 percent of that age group 10 years earlier. Reference: Industrial Relations Research Association, The Older Worker, 1988, pages 8 and 23.

6. True. The data indicates that the older the worker, the less likely he or she is to switch jobs. For example, occupational mobility rates for persons employed between January, 1982 and January, 1983 shows that men aged 35-45 years old had a 6.7% mobility rate compared to 4.8% for men 45-54 years old, 3.1% for those 55-64 and only 1.9% for workers 65 years and older. Reference: Current Population Survey, Bureau of Labor Statistics.

7. True. Education is the major influence affecting the probability of staying in the workforce vs. retiring. At ages 60-64, for example, college educated people are roughly twice as likely to be in the job market as are their least educated counterparts. Likewise, more educated persons, when working, are far more likely to do so on a full time year round basis. College graduates made up only 12% of the 65 and over population in 1986 but have more than double the proportion of full time year round workers. Reference: Industrial Relations Research Association, The Older Worker, 1988, page 34.

8. True. About a third of all older persons work after receiving a pension. Reference: Industrial Relations Research Association, The Older Worker, 1988, page 51.

9. False. According to a National academy of Sciences report, as persons age there is some reduction in pupil size together with a loss in accommodating capacity. The 20 year old eye receives about six times more light than the 80 year old eye in light adapted conditions. In dark adapted conditions, the younger eye receives 16 times more light. For any detailed task where performance varies with illumination, older workers will probably require extra lighting. Reference: National Research Council. Work, Aging and Vision: Report of a Conference, National Academy Press, 1987.

10. False. The majority of older workers are capable of changing to new conditions and situations. They adapt to many changes that occur such as moving to new homes, having children move away, and serious illnesses. Reference: American Association of Retired Persons, The Aging Work Force, page 33.

11. True. Older workers are generally less healthy, more impaired and functionally limited, and more disabled. This holds regardless of health measure used, whether it be condition classifications, indices of functional limitations, or self perceived classifications of disability. Of course, chronological age is not the best indication of the degenerative process for any particular individual. In addition, individuals might well compensate for these conditions in a variety of ways. Reference: Industrial Relations Research Association, The Older Worker, 1988, pages 90 and 108.

12. False. The 1982 Current Population Reports (U.S. Bureau of the Census, 1983) shows that only 3.3% of those 16-24 years old reported a work disability compared to 24.1% of workers between the ages of 55-64.

13. True. Older people do take longer to learn new materials compared to when they were younger or with performances of a younger person. However, many of these differences can be explained by variables other than age such as illness, motivation, learning style or lack of practice. All totaled, age is not a significant factor in the learning process. Reference: American Association of Retired Persons, The Aging Work Force, page 33.

14. False. A review of studies by Doering, Rhodes, and Schuster (1983) found mixed results. Some showed an improvement with age. For example, Maher (1955) found an improvement for salespeople and Holly et. al. (1978) found paraprofessionals improved with age. Older clerical workers were found to be more accurate and to have greater steadiness of output (Kutcher and Walker, 1960). Another study (Eisenberg, 1980) found that older examiners and material handlers in a garment manufacturing plant had higher productivity. On the other hand, decreases in productivity were reported in 15 studies. For scholars, engineers and scientists, the studies showed essentially an inverted U-shaped relationship between age and performance. Reference: Doering, Rhodes, and Schuster, The Aging Worker, Sage Publications, 1983.

15. True. Studies indicate that younger workers have higher injury frequency rates than do older workers. Reference: Dillingham, A., New Evidence on Age and Workplace Injuries, Industrial Gerontology, 1981, 4, 1-10.

16. True. While younger workers have a higher injury frequency rate than do older workers, older workers apparently have more serious injuries and lose more time per injury. The number of fatal accidents also increases with age. Reference: same reference as question 15.

17. True. Part time employment among the older population declined rather than increased between 1967 and 1986. Over this period, the proportion of older persons (55 plus) reporting either no employment or year round employment has risen gradually from 85.9% in 1967 to 89.2% in 1986. During 1886, approximately nine of every ten older persons in the U.S. either did not work at all or worked year-round. Reference: Ruhm, C. and Sum A., Job Stopping: The Changing Employment Patterns of Older Workers. In the Proceedings of the Forty-First Annual Meeting of the Industrial Relations Research Association, 1988, page 23.

18. True. Older people generally do have slower reaction times than do younger people, and this appears to be true regardless of the kind of reaction that is measured. However, the difference in reaction time is typically only a small fraction of a second, not enough to make a difference in performing most duties. Reference: American Association of Retired Persons, The Aging Workforce, page 34.

19. False. Career employment is a prevalent feature of U.S. labor markets. Almost two-thirds of household heads work in career jobs for more than 15 years and a fifth are employed by the same firm for more than 30 years. Only one in six works fewer than 10 years on a job. Reference: same as Question 17, page 24.

20. False. Most studies of taste and smell sensitivity show that they decrease with age. Indeed, all five senses tend to decline with age. Reference: same as Question 18, page 32.

Transcendus Exercise[1]

by Carole G. Parker
and Donald C. Klein

Administration Instructions

Goals:

1. To identify individual differences that may not be apparent among participants with respect to the nature and value of conflict

2. To increase awareness of participants' assumptions, beliefs, values, biases, concerns, and preferences in relation to conflict that results from their experiences with differences

3. To enable participants to manage more effectively their experience of diversity and conflict

Time Required:

50-60 Minutes

Materials:

Copies of the instructions for Transcendents and Earthings A copy of the Observer Role Sheet

Instructions:

The Transcendus Exercise provides a powerful opportunity for students to explore, confront, and challenge their assumptions and beliefs about the nature of conflict, its value, and even its inevitability in human relationships. There are two major roles to be played by participants in the Exercise:

1. **Transcendents:** inhabitants of a distant planet, who have come to Earth to find out more about the nature and purpose of conflict, which is unknown on their planet.

2. **Earthlings:** inhabitants of Earth, who have agreed to help educate their visitors from another planet about conflict.

The exercise is especially useful when it is embedded in a course, seminar, or workshop in which students can address the nature and management of differences and conflict both intellectually and experientially over time. It is not recommended as an isolated, single experience.

The exercise is most effective when neither Earthlings nor Transcendents are given information other than the background provided in their text. It is recommended that the roles for each group be provided on separate sheets of paper.

Participants are formed into groups of no less than six, no more than eight. Two members of each group become Transcendents; the rest are Earthlings. If ongoing groups in a class or workshop are used, Transcendents, once selected, are sent to Earthling groups other than their own.

Procedures:

1. Selection of Transcendents

The instructor nominates Transcendents based on his/her knowledge of individual class members and their ability to play the role.

The exercise encourages students to behave in unaccustomed ways, to set aside their ingrained assumptions and behavior regarding conflict, and to challenge one another's beliefs and actions. Therefore, it is advisable to introduce Transcendus only after a supportive learning climate has been created, students have had time to get to know each other, a good working relationship has been established between class members and the instructor, and the latter has developed sufficient familiarity with each person in the class.

The success of the exercise as a learning experience rests on the ability and willingness of those who play Transcendents to set aside their usual beliefs and to experiment with new patterns of behavior. However they are selected, therefore, it is important that they be comfortable with role playing, secure enough to play a role where they "let go" of their beliefs and notions about conflict, and flexible enough to appear strange or different. The most successful learning experience occurs when Transcendents are able to overcome any initial discomfort and the feeling that the exercise is silly or unrealistic.

If the assignment is explained carefully and discussed thoroughly with those nominated as Transcendents, those selected are most apt to enter wholeheartedly into the experience. In view of the special demands on them, it is important that they be given the opportunity to accept or decline the instructor's nomination once they understand and have had an opportunity to consider the nature of the assignment.

2. Preparation for Roles: 10-15 minutes

If possible, Transcendents should meet both as a total group and in pairs to prepare for their assignment. Once they have formed and are out of earshot of the Earthlings, they are provided with copies of the role instructions at the end of this section. At the same time each group of Earthlings meets to plan its strategy for how best to help their visitors learn about conflict. This effort requires students to address differing definitions of conflict and to explore various methods for introducing the idea to the visitors. Difficulties usually arise in arriving at consensus and group members often become impatient with and intolerant of one another. The instructor (and observers, if they are present) notes how the group handles such differences and later how they approach the task when the Transcendents are present. Observations are made available to the group during the debriefing of the exercise.

3. Meetings between Earthlings and Transcendents: 10-15 Minutes

Transcendent pairs join their assigned Earthling groups to begin discussion of the nature and purpose of conflict. These are leadership group discussions. No procedures, structures, or other guides are provided. The instructor may wish to prohibit physical violence and behavior that violates the personal privacy of fellow class members. If possible, the instructor circulates from group to group to observe samples of their interactions, record critical incidents, and note similarities and differences among the groups. These observations are shared with the class as appropriate in the final discussion of the exercise. The exercise is concluded when the instructor announces that the spaceship to Transcendus is ready to leave and all Transcendents must prepare to depart.

4. Total Class Reaction and Discussion: 30 Minutes

The entire class is reformed, if possible into one large circle, and members' reactions to the experience are solicited. At this point some Earthlings will have a strong need to describe the strategies they used and the frustrations they experienced when their efforts failed. Besides describing their own intentions, it is especially helpful at this point to encourage Earthlings to report on what they observed and experienced. They could also examine the differences among them with respect to their definitions of and feelings about conflict.

It is usually productive to ask class members to think about the differences between Earthlings and Transcendents. What was it, for example, which made it difficult, if not impossible, for the latter to understand what Earthlings have to say about conflict? Often the Transcendents themselves have their own insights to share about the shift in mind set that removed "conflict" from their way of construing events. It is often revealing to ask individual Transcendents to describe what it felt like to take the role of someone whose view of reality had no place for conflict.

Finally, it is recommended that those who were Earthlings be asked to examine their reactions to the differences between them and the Transcendents. Why was it so frustrating when the Transcendents could not understand? What kinds of feelings came to the surface? What kinds of judgments were made about these strangers who were so different?

Possible Learning Points

Versions of Transcendus have been used with learners of widely different ages, educational levels and backgrounds in seminars and workshops in several settings. With few exceptions, the experience engenders feelings of frustration for Earthlings, who soon discover that they cannot "get through" to the Transcendents, who - although fellow learners - are unable or unwilling to understand the most earnest explanations and demonstrations of conflict. Confronted by an orientation to conflict different from their own, Earthlings soon become confused and uncomfortable over their inability to communicate. Attempts often are made to trick the Transcendents into a conflict with the Earthlings. The Transcendents, by contrast, once they overcome their initial tension over taking on such an unusual role, typically become more relaxed, comfortably open in their ignorance and inability to understand, and often playful naive and transparently childlike. As one Earthling put it, "It felt like I was trying to explain something to a two-year old."

In every group of Earthlings there is at least one who escalates rapidly from disbelief, to mild frustration, irritation and downright anger. Others give up on the effort to bridge the difference between the two cultures and withdraw. Those who persist are unwilling to accept the possibility that the Transcendents' view of reality with respect to conflict is different and cannot be changed. To the bitter end they work very hard to convince the Transcendents that something is "wrong with them" because they have no experience of conflict. Almost inexorably the experience moves diversity and conflict from the realm of theory and abstract discussion to the plane of direct, undeniable reality. From the moment Earthling groups come together to figure out how to explain conflict to their visitors, students find themselves confronting substantial differences with respect both to their ways of defining conflict and the positive and negative values attached to it. Listed below are typical examples of definitions generated by Earthling groups about conflict:

1. Conflict exists when two or more parties want the same thing or their wants are incompatible in some way.

2. Conflict must involve emotionality; it is a disturbing emotion among two or more parties or within ourselves.

3. Conflict is a personal reaction involving negative feelings of anger and frustration.

4. The higher the stakes, the greater the conflict; you must care to have conflict.

5. Conflict can be within: oneself, a group, between groups.

6. Conflict involves competition: of wants; of viewpoints.

7. Conflict can be enjoyable.

The complexities and subtleties that surround the term "conflict" become even more inescapable as the Transcendents who, taking nothing for granted about the phenomenon, ask a continuing series of profoundly naive questions about what conflict is, under what circumstances it appears, why people get caught up in it, and what it has to offer them.

More than one Earthling has been touched in some deeply meaningful way by the childlike quality of the Transcendents. There are those who come to believe that conflict is, after all, a state of mind. Others become aware that to be in conflict they must be come prepared with the appropriate mind set or way of reacting. More than one Transcendent has reported that living in a conflict-free state has been a richly meaningful experience, one worth maintaining in "real life."

Variations:

1. Other methods for selecting Transcendents include:

   a. The students themselves choose from among their own groups once the exercise and the role of the Transcendents has been explained to them. Criteria for selection are developed by group members themselves. Often they include the degree to which individual members are interested in experiencing the role. We have been impressed and sometimes surprised by the ability of individuals to self-select and of group members to choose those well suited to the experience.

   b. Transcendents are randomly selected. Although simplest of all, leaving it to chance may be the most risky way because it increases the likelihood of discomfort, personal threat, and inability of role players to relinquish customary patterns of behavior and enter wholeheartedly into the experience of being Transcendents.

   c. Before the nature of the exercise is explained, volunteers are solicited from the class as a whole according to the general description, "Volunteer if you would enjoy stepping out of character and having fun playing the role of someone who comes from another planet." Although usually successful, a desirable safeguard is to enable anyone who seems more than usually threatened by the assignment to withdraw from the role once it has been explained and discussed with the instructor.

2. Debriefing Variations

Earthling groups and Transcendent pairs meet separately to discuss what they experienced, observed, and learned from the experience.

Fish Bowl: The class meets in a fish bowl pattern with the Transcendents sitting in the middle to discuss what they learned about conflict from their meetings with the Earthlings. An empty chair is available should an Earthling wish to contribute briefly to the discussion. Those who use the empty chair are instructed to make a brief comment and then vacate the seat to enable the Transcendents to go on with their discussion. Earthlings neither engage in dialogue nor interact with the Transcendents. It is helpful for the instructor to meet with the Transcendents to encourage exploration of specific material and help members of the group derive further learning from the experience.

The following questions are used to stimulate discussion in the fish bowl:

1. What happened?

2. What was the experience like for you?

3. What did you learn about conflict?

4. What do you want to take back to your planet?

5. What did you learn about differences?

3. Using Observers

If numbers in the class permit, it is useful to assign one or two observers to each group. This option is especially advised when an instructor wants to provide feedback to each group on their behavior during the exercise. It is extremely difficult for the instructor, who must divide attention among three or more groups, to provide useful feedback.

4. Video Taping

If possible, it may be useful to video tape the interactions between Earthlings and Transcendents and the debriefing. The tape can then be used for later analysis.

Reading Assignment

Assign "Distinguishing Difference and Conflicts" reading from the text book after the students have complete the Transcendus Exercise.

Notes

[1]The original version of the Transcendus Exercise was created by Donald Klein in June 1984 for use in the Beyond Conflict Training Laboratory in Bethel, Maine conducted by NTL Institute for Applied Behavioral Science.

Instructions for Observers

The task of the observer is to watch the behavior of group members and note how the group works together. Guidelines on what to look for include, but are not limited to, the following:

Observations	Transcendents	Earthlings
1. Who speaks most and least? In what order do people talk?		
2. Does everyone contribute? What happens to the contributions of different members?		
3. What occurs when the Transcendents arrive? To what extent does the group stick to its original plan for interacting with the visitors? Does the plan change? If so, how does the change occur?		
4. What is the level of tension in the group before the Transcendents arrive and after they join the group?		
5. What kinds of emotions are expressed by group members and exhibited in their posture, facial expressions, and actions?		
6. What were your thoughts as an individual sitting on the sidelines observing?		
7. What, if any, emotions were stirred in you as an observer?		

Instructions for Transcendents

You have been sent to Earth by the Governing Council of the planet "Transcendus" to study the Earthly phenomenon known as "conflict." You do not understand what is meant by the term and are completely ignorant about conflict in any form. The behavior known on Earth as conflict does not exist on Transcendus. The term "conflict" is not in the vocabulary or language of Transcendus. Other terms associated with conflict on Earth are also unfamiliar to you. Peace and harmony are the norms on your planet; difference and diversity are accepted and treated with appreciation. The idea of conflict is like a totally unfamiliar foreign language to you.

You are to function with a sincere attitude of inquiry. You have a serious job to do and much depends on your ability to carry out this assignment. You make contact with Earthlings with a genuine curiosity about this unfamiliar phenomenon. You are prepared to ask questions, seek explanations, gather information and make observations. You are prepared in every way possible to decide what "conflict" is and prepared to take this information back to your planet.

It is entirely possible that, despite the Earthlings' best efforts to help you, it will turn out that "conflict" makes no sense to you. No matter. You remain within your accustomed state of peace and harmony although you cannot make sense of what the Earthlings say or do in their efforts to explain.

Instructions for Earthlings

As representatives of Earth, you have agreed to help the Transcendents. You are experts on conflict, having experienced, observed, and lived with it all your lives. Your visitors want to know what conflict is and what purposes it serves, if any. Your job is to do whatever you can to educate the Transcendents about conflict. Because you take conflict for granted and probably experience it almost on a daily basis, it may be difficult for you to understand how any society of intelligent, thinking beings can exist without experiencing conflict or understanding what is meant by the term. Using your skills in conflict, which you have been developing throughout your lives, you want to provide the Transcendents with the unique opportunity to learn and understand as much about this Earthly phenomenon as possible.

You may use whatever methods you deem appropriate to convey this idea to your guests. It is important, however, to keep in mind that it is not part of your job to persuade the Transcendents that conflict already exists on their planet. Their question is whether conflict is worth importing into their home planet. Do your best to help them understand what conflict is and what purposes it serves on Earth.

Gender and Participation: An Exploration of Differences

by Joan V. Gallos

Administration Instructions

Goals:

1. To explore the connections between gender and task group participation

2. To examine student perceptions about gender-based behaviors

3. To provide opportunities for students to identify and explore the gender stereotypes that they hold

4. To examine the power and consequences of attributing motivation to others for their behavior

Time Required:

90 minutes is preferred (although the activity can be successfully run in 60 minutes by limiting the number of observer comments)

Materials:

Observer worksheets in student text book, copies of character description sheets from teacher's manual, a topic for group discussion, a class-related group project, or materials for a simple group ranking task

Physical Setting Requirements:

This activity works best in a room with flexible seating where a "fishbowl" setting can be arranged. The task group can work around a table or desk, or can be seated in a circle of chairs. Whatever the arrangement, it is critical that observers be able to see and hear all that goes on in the task group.

Instructions:

1. Instructors should begin by explaining to students that this is a role playing activity designed to explore beliefs about gender and group participation and that six to eight student volunteers, balanced between men and women, will be needed to participate in a group task. The task will be assigned by the instructor and the group will be observed by the class while performing its task.

   [This activity can be run with as few as five volunteers or as many as ten, duplicating character descriptions if necessary. The critical factor in determining the number of role players is class size: the activity needs at least as many observers as role players.]

2. Once volunteers have been determined, the instructor should distribute a different character description sheet to each student. Character description sheets are provided for nine different role players. For copying convenience, several roles were placed on each sheet. Be sure to cut them apart before distributing to students.

   Character descriptions A, B or C should be assigned to male volunteers. These descriptions are based on conversation styles, involvement patterns, and/or comfort levels historically associated with men.

Character descriptions D, E, F, or G should be assigned to female volunteers. These descriptions are based on conversation styles, involvement patterns, and/or comfort levels historically associated with women.

Character descriptions H and I can be assigned to either men or women.

3. Students should be advised not to share information about their characters or roles with each other or with the larger class, but to use the information to inform their involvement in the task group. Students should be told that their role descriptions contain characteristics, identified from the research literature, about differences among men and women in participation styles, involvement, and comfort levels in mixed-gender task and discussion groups, and that the roles have been constructed to emphasize different behaviors and attitudes.

4. Student participants in the task group should be given time alone to study their roles and become comfortable with their characters before they receive the assigned task. This preparation can be done while the instructor explains the role of observer to the rest of the class. They should be advised to interact with others as realistically as possible during the task group while remaining consistent with their assigned character descriptions. (It is easy for students in their anxiety to play exaggerated caricatures of their roles. This can be entertaining but less helpful in generating later discussion.)

5. Students who have not been assigned character descriptions will observe the task group in action and record their observations about (a) what they see happening in the group and (b) how they see individuals behaving. These observations will be written in columns 1 and 2 on the provided worksheets.

   Instructors will want to explain in detail the use of the observer worksheets, stressing the importance of recording notes about who observers have watched and what they have seen in order to provide descriptive and specific feedback later. For groups new to process observation, instructors may want to assign specific observers to watch certain participants and to review rules for effective feedback.

   Observers also need to be clear about the fact that they will be given time before reporting out to review their observations and to make notes (in column 3 on their observer worksheet) about possible explanations for observed behaviors. Observers are easily confused about this and can become frustrated trying to watch the action in the task group while they struggle to fill in column 3 on the worksheet.

6. When observers and task group participants are ready, the instructor should create a "fishbowl" arrangement and announce the assigned task.

   One possible task is a simple group ranking activity. For example, "Lost on the Moon" or any of its variations works well. Alternatively, instructors may want to create their own list of activities or characteristics to rank, or prepare a group assignment more directly connected to a class topic, activity, or reading. For example, in a discussion of a case situation, questions about an assigned reading or topic, or preparation for a class decision or project or an exercise from the student text are all possible group tasks. The critical factor in the choice of task is providing opportunities for participants to interact with each other for about 10 to 15 minutes.

7. The group task should run no longer than 15 minutes. After that, observers become overwhelmed with information and forget specific group events so that the quality of feedback and discussion deteriorates. Groups will probably not complete the assigned task in the allotted time. That is expected, although it may tempt task group members to use feedback time to continue their task work. Instructors should be prepared to intervene if conversation flows back to task content and away from observations about group process.

8. After stopping the group task, instructors should ask group participants to take a few moments and make some notes for themselves about what they saw happening and why. At the same time, observers can review their observations and make similar notes about how to account for what they saw (i.e., comments for column 3 on the observer worksheet).

Taking time to have participants and observers alike make notes improves the quality of the feedback and gives all an opportunity to switch gears for the processing.

9. Student observers now share their recorded observations and explanations with the large group. Depending on class size, this can be done with volunteers or by going around the room and asking everyone to share their most critical observations.

    It is important again to have students focus on individual behavior. Instructors should push students to "own" their explanations for why they thought things happened as they did in anticipation of the later discussion on assumptions and attri*butions.*

    Group participants can be asked to share their observations and explanations, although advised not to reveal their character descriptions yet.

10. When observers and participants have fully shared what they saw happening and why, task group participants should reveal their assigned roles and characters.

11. A simple question, such as "Having now heard the roles that people played, were there any surprises?" will easily begin discussion.

    The revelation of the assigned character descriptions is often powerful for students. Many of their attributions and interpretations are inaccurate or based on widely shared gender stereotypes.

    For example, students often assume that role player D is confident, involved and "with it" and are shocked to find that head nodding and smiles are camouflage for insecurity - a role which research tells us women can easily find themselves playing in mixed-gender tasks groups and discussions. Alternatively, observers are sure that role player F is confident and self-assured and are equally shocked to find confident aggression as another screen to mask deep fears.

    The observations and surprises lead to good discussion about the stereotypes that people hold and about the power of the attributions made from observing others in action.

    Instructors will want to acknowledge that although the character descriptions, by necessity, stress only one or two behaviors, they are grounded in knowledge of historic patterns associated with men and women. Instructors should probe specifically into the observations about gender and be prepared to discuss the research base behind the portraits.

Readings that may help instructors prepare for this include:

M. Belenky, B. Clinchy, N. Goldberger, and J. Tarule. Women's Way of Knowing: *The Development of Self, Voice, and Mind*. New York: Basic Books, 1986.

J. Gallos. "Women's Experiences and Ways of Knowing: Implications for Teaching and Learning in the Organizational Behavior Classroom." Journal of Management Education, XVII:1, February 1993.

D. Tannen. You Just Don't Understand: Women and Men in Conversation. New York: Morrow, 1990.

Possible discussion questions might include items such as:

1. What can we learn about how our stereotypes influence our perceptions of men and women in groups?

2. How do our attributions, the things we imagine others are thinking and feeling, influence our interactions in groups?

3. If making attributions is a natural process that we all use to make sense of what we see, how could we test to make sure that our attributions are on target?

4. What can we learn about how gender affects group participation?

5. How did gender affect your involvement in this activity today?

6. What have people learned from this activity about how they might increase their own effectiveness in groups?

VARIATION: *Gender, Participation, and the College Classroom*

This activity can easily be adapted to look at gender differences at the classroom level rather than in small task groups.

For that focus, one student is selected to prepare and present a brief, 5 minute presentation on a topic of his/her choice to a small group of students. Depending on the confidence and sophistication of the selected student presenter, instructors can assign the preparation *for this presentation* days ahead of time or allow 10-15 minutes in-class time for the presenter while other students explore and learn about their participant or observer roles.

A small group of students is then selected to play the role of the classroom audience. They are given character descriptions similar to those in the gender and participation activity as described above. This time, however, the participants use their character descriptions to inform how they would behave in the lecture and interact with the presenter/instructor.

For example, student A would assume the role of seriously questioning the validity of propositions presented by the instructor. Student B would listen carefully, awestruck by the experience and expertise of the speaker, and take down every word, etc. Teachers interested in a classroom level focus may want to rewrite the role descriptions accordingly.

Other students in the class again become observers, recording both (a) what they see happening between the instructor and audience and (b) how they might account for these behaviors.

Teachers using this focus will follow a similar sequence of soliciting observations and explanations from observers, asking the audience role players to reveal their characters, and discussing the observations, perceptions, and attributions. They will also want to explore the broader implications of these issues for learning and participation in their own classroom.

A suggested way to explore these issues is through the creation of small groups to examine questions like: *(a) In what ways do the issues we have just seen in this role play mirror what happens in our own classroom? (b) how do these issues affect your participation in this class? (c) how do they affect your learning? (d) what can we do in light of these issues to maximize student learning?* Teachers can ask small groups to report out their findings or can conduct a large group discussion about the issues.

Gender and Participation: *An Exploration of Differences*

Character Description: Participant Role A

Your role in this task group is to seriously question the validity of the propositions and suggestions presented by your fellow participants. Accuracy of information is most critical to you.

You will want to ask for evidence, additional proof, references, information about their experiences or credentials, and so on.

You have recently read a number of books on this subject which present a very different perspective from many of the suggestions that others are making. You think others are wrong and that you have important and relevant information to share with the group.

✂ —

Gender and Participation: An Exploration of Differences

Character Description: Participant Role B

Your role in this task group is to ignore or disagree with whatever the women in the group say. You believe the women present do not have the relevant experience or expertise that the male participants have. You respect experience and expertise more than anything else, and think those without it should remain silent and defer to those more experienced. You, therefore, feel free to interrupt the women, change any topic of conversation that they introduce, or actively disagree with their positions.

You address direct comments only to other male students.

Gender and Participation: *An Exploration of Differences*

Character Description: Participant Role C

Your role in this task group is to demonstrate to others your knowledge and expertise on the topic. You feel entitled to speak whenever something important comes to mind. You like to engage others whom you respect in public conversations about your interests or experiences. You don't mind interrupting others. You like to play devil's advocate and question others. You feel annoyed at those who try to dominate the conversation. You can feel very competitive with others.

✂--

Gender and Participation: *An Exploration of Differences*

Character Description: Participant Role D

Your role in this task group is to actively participate as long as the environment is comfortable for you. You are most comfortable in a group when you feel listened to, responded to, and validated. If you feel ignored or threatened, you withdraw. Withdrawal behavior for you means that you continue to look pleasant and involved through smiles, head nods, and other non-verbals. You continue to makes notes for yourself. In fact, because of your increasing discomfort, listening and note taking become more challenging for you.

Gender and Participation: *An Exploration of Differences*

Character Description: Participant Role E

Your role in this task group is to listen carefully to others. You admire and are somewhat awestruck by the experience and expertise of your fellow students. You want to take down almost every important word that they say. You are pleased to have the opportunity to be a part of this task group. You are annoyed because some people keep interrupting folks who seem to know what they are talking about. You don't want to speak out to quiet the interrupters because that's just not your style. You also realize that joining the debate will further prevent the group from finishing its task.

Your rising anger, however, is making it difficult to focus on the topic being discussed.

✄ —

Gender and Participation: *An Exploration of Differences*

Character Description: Participant Role F

You are not sure why you have been included in this task group. You have doubts about your own abilities, and are sure that everyone else in the classroom has more experience and expertise than you. You fear that others may recognize this too. You have decided that the best course of action for you is to prove you really belong. You brag about yourself and your expertise. You compete with others for air time. You ask questions. You argue. You evaluate other's positions. You try to cover your fears by being a highly active participant.

Your fears, however, make listening to others difficult. For that reason, you often misunderstand key points or interrupt before others have clearly finished their argument.

Gender and Participation: An Exploration of Differences

Character Description: Participant Role G

You learn best when you have opportunities to connect what you hear with your personal experiences. Because you are relatively new in the workplace, you don't always have examples that tie directly to organizational or managerial experiences. You believe, however, that your broader life experience examples (like discussions about home or friends or family) are relevant and essential to clarifying the points expressed by others in the discussion.

You feel comfortable talking about yourself, expressing your feelings, and sharing your reactions to the topic, the task, and the group's dynamics.

✂ –

Gender and Participation: *An Exploration of Differences*

Character Description: Participant Role H

Your role in this task group is to support the people that you see as the real experts in this group by asking questions and bringing the action back to them whenever anyone interrupts and tries to sway the conversation away from their intended direction.

You value the experts' expertise and want the full benefit of their experience. You try hard to facilitate the presentation in any positive way you can design.

Gender and Participation: *An Exploration of Differences*

Character Description: Participant Role I

You are not sure why you have been included in this task group. You have doubts about your own abilities, and are sure that everyone else in the group has more experience and expertise than you. You fear that if you speak, others will recognize this too.

You have decided that the best course of action for you is to remain silent but to look engaged. You will not take initiatives until someone calls on you. Fear that someone might call on you, however, makes listening difficult.

The In-Basket Dilemma

by Alice L. O'Neill

Administration Instructions

Goals:

1. To make students aware of the effects of multicultural issues on the practice of management

2. To help students recognize special management issues in the health care setting

3. To help students recognize the positive effects of group management decisions and actions

Time Required:

If prioritization is accomplished by each student prior to class time, one-half hour of class time should be utilized for small groups to rank management actions and discuss why they chose their rankings. Class discussion can then be led by the instructor about each group's prioritization methods and reasons for the rankings.

Materials:

Pens or pencils and Table II from student text.

Instructions:

There is no one best prioritization list, and some of the messages may be handled concomitantly (Ms. Roth is involved in several of the messages, therefore Mike Flynn can begin to address those problems in a single meeting with her).

It would be helpful if a long-term care administrator (NHA) could address the class at some time to illustrate the issues faced in health care administrator decisions, especially those in the long-term care setting.

A unified ranking of action priorities must be accomplished by each group. "Dissenters" may document their reasons; however, group consensus is important.

Sequencing the items:

Although there is no "right sequencing" of the items, students should recognize that some problems are more urgent than others and that some messages can be handled concomitantly with one meeting and/or telephone call.

Answers to Discussion Questions

1. What are the diversity issues in this In-Basket exercise? "Work ethic" - what is it and does it differ by culture?

- Single parent difficulty with babysitters and work schedules

- Language barriers

- Economic/financial situations of diverse groups

- Likes and dislikes (food)

- Approaches to treatment for health care needs and showing emotions (pain, etc.) differ by cultural group

- Referring to employees as "Girls"

- Cultural differences between minority groups

- AIDS, homosexuality and health care/employment

- Religion and employment

- Wages of diverse minority groups

2. What diverse groups are represented?

- Single white administrator of predominately female employee component

- Female employee

- Black resident

- Hispanic resident

- Economically/financially depressed

- Nursing home residents

- Chinese/Italian residents (multi-ethnic)

- Hispanic nursing assistants

- AIDS patients and employees

- Homosexuals

- Religious groups

3. What legal problems may arise from some of the diversity issues presented?

- Slander if allegations untrue

- Theft of a resident's personal belongings, if allegations true

- Transfer or assignment of a patient to another room because of race, ethnicity, etc. is illegal and in addition, the facility could lose Medicare and Medical Assistance funding

- Invasion of privacy - searching patient's personal belongings without consent

- Liability of Board, administrator and employees involved in several of the instances

- Union activity - what the facility can and cannot do legally during union activity such as this

- Disregarding resident likes and dislikes takes away a resident's personal right of choice, and may be considered patient abuse

- Patient transfer because hospital does "not want him in our facility"; hospital must be able to show inability to care for the resident's needs (facilities should be able to care for most residents who have chronic communicable diseases)

- Sexual harassment

- Employee discrimination because of religious beliefs

4. What are some major differences between Northwood Community Hospital and Birch Acres?

Type of patient served, diseases and problems of residents and patients, resident length of stay in facility, rules and regulations about facility operations, geographic location, types of minority groups in the area, presence of union, more managers to handle problems in an acute care setting, wage and benefit levels, employee component makeup, relationship with residents, families and community, necessity of nursing assistant, certification, reimbursement and other financial considerations differ. (Several more may be appropriately discussed).

5. What might Mike Flynn have failed to do before he accepted the job at Birch Acres?

Failed to investigate the geographic location and its ethnic differences; failed to distinguish the differences between acute and long-term care administration; failed to make himself aware of the effects that diversity issues can have on health care administration decisions.

6. What actions should be taken to help overcome staffing problems and employee concerns? Who should take these actions?

- Improve staff morale (discuss various methods in class)

- Continuing education seminars for nurse managers

- Provide inservices to staff about AIDS, resident rights, infection control procedures, and cultural diversity issues.

- Establish measures to keep good staff

- The Board, administrator, and all managers should take these actions.

7. What can be done to address the evident problems of residents who are roommates and cannot get along satisfactorily?

Although it is not legal to assign residents to rooms of the basis of race, religion, color, etc. (in most instances), it is advisable to determine if roommate personalities will "clash"; if one roommate likes to retire early for sleep, you would not want to place that person in a room with someone who likes to watch the late night TV show. Common sense should be used in room placement and accommodations made whenever possible - remember that many of these residents will spend the rest of their lives in the facility.

Multicultural Negotiations Exercise

by Egidio A. Diodati

Administration Instructions

Goals:

1. To allow the students to experience the frustration resulting from, what must be termed, a clash of cultures.

2. To appreciate the problems associated with negotiating with people of other cultures.

The Japanese team instructions are clear that they remain almost completely stoic in the face of anything that these American barbarians may do or say. This, they believe will, in the long run get them the very best deal. The American team is here to close the deal in record time. Each member of the American team has a personal (career driven) and a corporate investment in closing this deal as soon as possible.

The results of this clash, if the role play does not break down, will be that the American team will know exactly what most Americans have learned about international negotiations - a lack of knowledge about the other's culture will put you at a distinct disadvantage.

Time Required:

With some advance planning, this exercise can usually be completed in about an hour.

Materials:

Copies of instructions for the American and Japanese teams from the teacher's manual, feedback sheets and student instructions from the student's text, pencils, pens, a rectangular table with 8 chairs and name tags for the American and Japanese team members.

Instructions:

1. In order to minimize the time needed, the room should be set up for the negotiation session in advance using a rectangular table with four seats on each side. The Japanese side should have three chairs at the table with one chair set up behind the three. The American side of the tableshould have four chairs side-by-side.

2. At the beginning of the exercise, ask for eight volunteers from the class. The eight people will role play two negotiation teams, while the remainder of the class observes the negotiations. The role play takes place at the headquarters of a Japanese automobile manufacturer. The American team has come to sell microchips and other components to the Japanese company.

3. The volunteers should be divided up into the two teams of four and separated into two rooms if possible. (If not, they should, at least, be out of hearing range of each other.) They are then given their instruction sheets. Neither team can have access to the other's instruction sheets. After dividing up the particular roles, the teams should meet for 10 - 15 minutes to develop their negotiation strategy.

4. After the preparation time is over, the Japanese team should enter the room first, since they must greet the Americans when they arrive. At this point, the Americans should be brought in and the role play begins. Time for the negotiations should be 20 - 30 minutes. The rest of the class should be told that their role is to observe and their observations will be part of the discussion of the responses.

Some things which are critical to the exercise are:

- The competing teams must not have any knowledge of the instructions given to the other team

- Both teams must be convinced to stay "in role" in order to maximize the benefit of the exercise

- The American team must be convinced that they are there to champion the interests of their nation (economically), company (financially), and their own careers

- The Japanese team must be convinced that although they are dealing with barbarians, they must be polite to them. Even though women and minorities really have no place in business negotiations, the Japanese team will, within certain bounds, tolerate their presence

5. After the role play, the members of each team and the observers complete the feedback sheets in the text.

At this point it is very beneficial to record the responses on the board. Since the questions are similar on each of the Feedback Sheets, the differences in the responses will be driven by the students' different positions in the role play and should highlight the degree of cultural diversity.

Instructions for the Japanese Team
(To be copied and distributed to the members of the Japanese Team only.)

Goals:

As members of the "buying" organization you have the power in these negotiations. By showing no emotion or indication of commitment, it is your goal to wear the Americans down as they attempt to "close" the deal. You know that by dragging out these negotiations as long as possible, you will get them to offer you their best deal.

Instructions:

The Japanese team should be comprised of only men. The negotiations are taking place at the corporate headquarters of a Japanese automobile manufacturer. The American team has just arrived at the location to begin an effort to get the Japanese automobile manufacturer to buy electrical computerized subcomponents which are manufactured in the United States.

Composition of the Japanese Team is:

- one senior executive, **Mr. Ozaka**. He is the real decision maker and during the negotiation session says nothing. He is given no special treatment by the other members of the team. He sits behind the other team members and is not looked at or spoken to by his team. He shows no emotion through-out the entire exercise. He may be interested in this product but believes by making the Americans come back a second time, he will get a better deal.

- two middle managers, **Mr. Nishimuro** and **Mr. Sheno**, who sit opposite the Americans but pretend to have no English skills. From time to time they may turn to each other and whisper, but nothing else. They have been ordered to this meeting by Mr. Ozaka but know of his disdain for the Americans, since he believes that they are too loud and aggressive for civil people.

- a low level manager, **Mr. Kawazaka**, who conducts all of the communication with the Americans and is required to sit the nearest to them. It is Mr. Kawazaka's role to greet the Americans in English and to introduce them to the other members. Mr. Kawazaka has no power in the negotiations whatsoever but believes that he is obligated to be pleasant to these foreigners.

When the Americans enter the negotiation room, they are pleasantly greeted by Mr. Kawazaka. However, Mr. Ozaka, Mr. Nishimuro, and Mr. Sheno stand, bow slightly and then hand their business cards to the Americans when they are introduced. Any women or other minority members of the American team will not receive business cards or be bowed to as deeply as the other members of the American team.

During the negotiations, only Mr. Kawazaka will talk with the Americans. However, when listening to whatever the Americans have to say, he may only say "hai" and bow (with a less deep bow to the women and minority members of the American team). Conversation by Mr. Kawazaka with the Americans, beyond that point, should be limited to clarifying comments which basically restate the American position. Whenever the Americans try to close the deal, Mr. Kawazaka's only comment should be, "That is very interesting. We will consider this and get back to you". From time to time he may have whispered conversations with Mr. Nishimuro and Mr. Sheno.

Instructions for the American Team

(To be copied and distributed to members of the American team only.)

Goals:

Mr. Jones and his team are here to open up the Japanese market for their company. It is critical to the financial well being of the company and, more importantly, to the individual careers of the team members that this contract be closed as soon as possible.

Instructions:

The American Team will be comprised of at least one woman and have a multi-racial mix, if possible. There will be a leader and three followers of equal rank, with each of the three having different sales responsibilities. The leader should do most of the talking during the negotiations, only referring to the three associates when their expertise is needed.

Team Leader - **Mr. Jones**, Senior Vice-President of Worldwide Sales for Acme Microchip Corp. He is newly appointed to this position and has been promised a seat on the Board of Directors if he can open up the Japanese market. He knows that the Japanese use a similar type of mini-computer in their manufacturing and he knows that with some cost cutting, Acme can produce it as cheaply as they. Closing this deal is a must for his future at Acme.

Manufacturing Engineer - **Mr./Ms. Smith** has a Masters Degree in Electrical Engineering from Cal. Tech. and has met engineers from the Japanese company an various conferences. Through conversations with them, he knows that they are looking for an outside supplier for this particular component. If he can play a strong role in closing this deal, Mr. Jones has promised him a promotion to Director of International Manufacturing.

Marketing Analyst - **Mr./Ms. Nelson** has an MBA from UCLA with a specialty in pricing this type of product for international markets. Mr./Ms. Nelson has been negotiating quite successfully with various European car companies for this type of product and knows that price is always a driving factor. His/her research indicates that, while Acme is producing this component for a unit cost $12.50, it is costing the Japanese at least $14.25 each. Although his starting point for negotiations with the Japanese is in the $13.50 to $13.75 range, he would (with permission from Mr. Jones) go as low as $13.00 for a large quantity order. He really believes that they would jump on a $13.00/unit price.

Account Executive - **Mr./Ms. Frost** has been with the company for 5 years, since graduating from a small liberal arts college on the east coast. Although he/she has done very well in income the past two years, he sees this as an opportunity to show how much he knows about closing business and plans to bring home the business with a stellar performance at these negotiations. He/she sees this as an "up or out" move. If he cannot close this deal, he may have to go elsewhere for upward mobility.

Create An Exercise

by June Allard

Administration Instructions

Goal:

To help students gain greater information about, and understanding of, physical and mental disabilities.

Time Required:

Day of assignment: 10-15 minutes to form groups and explain the assignment

Due Date: entire class period; perhaps two class periods depending upon number and complexity of exercises

Materials:

Student Instructions and Worksheets from text, pens or pencils. Copies of Exercise Rating Sheet (optional) from Teacher's Manual.

Instructions:

1. Instruct students to form groups (or assign them to groups) of five or six members each. Tell students to list the members of their group on their worksheets. (Note. They may also wish to list phone numbers as well).

2. Instruct groups to create an exercise designed to demonstrate/experience a physical or mental disability. Assign a different disability to each group so that the entire class will be exposed to a range of

3. The exercise can take the form of a demonstration, role play, simulation, or game such as a board game, word game, trivia, or whatever. It can be designed for individuals, small groups or large groups. Stress that it cover a broad range of information pertinent to the topic.

All appropriate materials such as: introduction, rules, game board and pieces, props, scoring sheets, note-taking sheets or forms or whatever is needed for the exercise are to be included.

4. Review the criteria to be used to grade the exercise which include:

       a) accuracy of information used

       b) breadth of coverage of content

       c) evidence that course material has been reviewed and organized (e.g., development of meaningful game categories or roles, including more than a small sampling of course material)

       d) evidence that additional material has been obtained on the disability, e.g., references) neatness, completeness and coherence of materials (e.g., readable instructions, meaningful introduction, usable game or observational materials, etc.)

5. Discuss possible sources of information on disabilities (library, disability associations, interviews with the disabled, etc.)

6. Tell students to enter the assignment due date on their instruction sheets and plan to play/demonstrate their exercises in class on that date.

Optional Assignments

This exercise can also be used for other aspects of diversity by assigning students to create an exercise on gender, racial, and ethnic differences, age or sexual orientation.

Assign a paper describing the information sources used, rationale for type of exercise designed, and discussion of what the group learned while creating the exercise.

When the exercises are presented to the class, student groups can rate or grade those designed by other groups using the criteria given for designing the exercises. This helps to ensure greater attention to the material presented on disabilities by other groups.

The Exercise Rating Sheet on the next page may be reproduced for this purpose. Each group will need a separate rating sheet for each other group. The instructor should allow time for group discussion on the ratings of the exercises. Student groups may also be graded on the quality of their comments and evaluations of the exercises. For this purpose, a space had been provided for the names of the evaluators.

Create an Exercise
Exercise Rating Sheet

Evaluation of Group: _____ Exercise Title:_____

	E		D			C			B			A	
Accuracy of Information	0	1	2	3	4	5	6	7	8	9	10	11	12

Content Coverage	0	1	2	3	4	5	6	7	8	9	10	11	12

Course Material	0	1	2	3	4	5	6	7	8	9	10	11	12

Additional Material	0	1	2	3	4	5	6	7	8	9	10	11	12

Completeness & Coherence	0	1	2	3	4	5	6	7	8	9	10	11	12

Overall Evaluation	0	1	2	3	4	5	6	7	8	9	10	11	12

General Comments:

Evaluators:

SECTION V
Additional Resource Material

Recent Materials on Understanding Diversity

Part I
On Understanding Diversity

Books

Cox, Taylor Jr. Cultural Diversity in Organizations: Theory, Research & Practice. San Francisco: Berrett-Koehler Publishers, 1993.

Griesman, Eugene B. Diversity: Challenges and Opportunities. New York: HarperCollins College Publishers, 1993.

Lamont, Michele & Fournier, Marcel, editors. Cultivating Differences: Symbolic Boundaries & the Making of Inequality. Chicago: University of Chicago Press, 1992.

Locke, Don C. Increasing Multicultural Understanding: A Comprehensive Model. Newbury Park CA: Sage, 1992.

Saxonhouse, Arlene W. The Birth of Political Science in Ancient Greek Thought. Chicago: University of Chicago Press, 1992.

Videos

A Tale of "O" - a highly effective video on being different in the workplace. Available in both Spanish and English from Goodmeasure, Inc., One Memorial Drive, Cambridge, MA 02142, (617) 621-3838.

Part II
On Organization and Diversity

Books

Fernandez, John P. Managing a Diverse Workforce: Regaining the Competitive Edge., Lexington, MA: Lexington Books, 1991.

Eloshmoivi, Farid & Harris, Philip R. Multicultural Management: New Skills for Global Success., Houston, TX: Gulf Publishing, 1993.

Gardenswartz, Lee & Rowe, Anita. Managing Diversity: A Complete Desk Reference & Planning Guide. Homewood, Il: Business One Irwin San Diego, Pfeiffer & Co., 1993.

Harris, Philip R. & Moran, Robert T. Managing Cultural Differences. 3rd ed, Houston TX: Gulf Publishing, 1991.

Jackson, Susan E. & Associates. Diversity in the Workplace. NY: The Guilford Press, 1992.

Jamieson, David & O'Mara, Julie. Managing Workforce 2000. San Francisco: Jossey-Bass, 1991.

Morrison, Ann M. & Crabtree Kristen M. Developing Diversity in Organizations: A Digest of Selected Literature. Greensboro, NC: Center for Creative Leadership, 1992.

Morrison, Ann M. (1992). The New Leaders: Guidelines on leadership diversity in America, San Francisco: Jossey-Bass.

Simmons, George F. Vazquez, Carmen & Harris R. Philip. <u>Transcultural Leadership: Empowering the Diverse Work Force</u>. Houston TX: Gulf Publishing, 1993.

Thiederman, Sandra. <u>Profiting in America's Multicultural Marketplace: How to Do Business Across Cultural Lines</u>. Lexington Books, 1992.

Thiederman, Sandra. <u>Bridging Cultural Barriers for Corporate Success: How to Manage the Multicultural Workforce</u>. Lexington Books, 1990.

Videos

<u>Affirmative Action for Men</u>. Available from Films for the Humanities & Sciences, P.O. Box 2053, Princeton, NJ 08543-2053, (609) 452-1128.

<u>Employer versus Employee</u> - a woman sues IBM for wrongful discharge. Available from Films for the Humanities & Sciences, P.O. Box 2053, Princeton, NJ 08543-2053, (609) 452-1128.

<u>Sexual Harassment in the Workplace</u>, <u>Sexual Harassment from 9 to 5</u>, <u>Sexual Harassment in the Job</u>, and <u>Sexual Harassment of Men by Women</u>. Available from Films for the Humanities & Sciences, P.O. Box 2053, Princeton, NJ 08543-2053, (609) 452-1128.

<u>Sexual Harassment: It's Not Just Courtesy - It's the Law</u> & <u>Sexual Harassment is Bad Business</u>. Available from Insight Media, 1231 W. 85th Street, New York, NY, 10024, (212) 721-6316.

<u>Valuing Diversity</u> - series of award winning video tapes. Produced by Griggs Productions, 2046 Clement St., San Francisco, CA 94121-2118, (415) 668-4200.

<u>Women at the Top</u>, <u>Women & the Corporate Game</u>, <u>Women Against Women</u>, <u>Can Working Women Have it All?</u>, & <u>Women in the Boardroom</u>. Available from Films for the Humanities & Sciences, P.O. Box 2053, Princeton, NJ 08543-2053, (609) 452-1128.

<u>The Mosaic Workplace</u> - 10 part diversity series available as single titles or as a set:

- <u>Why Value Diversity</u>

- <u>Understanding Our Biases & Assumptions</u>

- <u>Men & Women Working Together</u>

- <u>Sexual Harassment</u>

- <u>Recruiting & Interviewing</u>

- <u>Helping New Employees Feel Valued</u>

- <u>Understanding Different Cultural Values & Styles</u>

- <u>Meeting the Diversity Challenge</u>

- <u>Success Strategies for Minorities</u>

- <u>The Future is Now Celebrating Diversity</u>

Available from Films for the Humanities & Sciences, P.O. Box 2053, Princeton, NJ 08543-2053, (609) 452-1128.

Newsletter

Managing Diversity - a monthly newsletter of information for people interested in Diversity issues. Subscription information available from Managing Diversity, JALMC, P.O. Box 819, Jamestown, NY 14702-0809.

Part III
On the Dimensions of Diversity

Books

DeFreitas, George. Inequality at Work: Hispanics in the U.S. Labor Force. NY: Oxford University Press, 1991.

Fagenson, Ellen S. Women in Management. vol 4. Thousand Oaks, CA: Sage Publications, 1993.

Greenberg, David F. The Construction of Homosexuality. Chicago: University of Chicago Press, 1988.

Jones, Timothy L. The Americans with Disabilities Act: A Review of Best Practices. New York: American Management Association, 1993.

Knause, Stephen B., Rosenfeld, Paul & Culbertson, Amy, editors. Hispanics in the Workplace. Newbury Park, CA: Sage Publications, 1992.

Konek, Carol Wolfe & Kitch, Sally L. Women and Careers. Thousand Oaks, CA: Sage Publications, 1993.

Malson, Micheline R., Mudimbe-Boyr, Elizabeth, O'Barr, Jean F. & Wyer, Mary. Black Women in America. Chicago: University of Illinois Press, 1990.

Monk, Richard C., Taking Sides: Clashing Views on controversial Issues in Race & Ethnicity. 1st ed. Guilford, CT: Dushkin Publishing, 1993.

Nagler, Mark, ed., Perspectives on Disability. Palo Alto, CA: Health Markets Research, 1993.

Powell, Gary N. Women & Men in Management. Thousand Oaks, CA: Sage Publications, 1993.

Videos - Gender

Women Managing Men, Leading Women, Leading Men, Videos available from Insight Media, 121 W 85th St., New York, NY 10024, (212) 721-6316.

Sexual Stereotypes in Media: Superman & the Bride. Video on the influence of media images on gender stereotypes. Available from Films for the Humanities & Sciences, P.O. Box 2053, Princeton, NJ 08543-2053, (609) 452-1128.

Stale Roles and Tight Buns, a video on the stereotyping of American men. Available from O.A.S.I.S., 15 Willoughby St., Boston, MA 02135, (617) 782-7769.

Videos -Race/Ethnicity

<u>Latino Employment & Unemployment</u>. Available from Films for the Humanities & Sciences, P.O. Box 2053, Princeton, NJ 08543-2053, (609) 452-1128.

<u>Black Urban Professionals</u>. Available from Films for the Humanities & Sciences, P.O. Box 2053, Princeton, NJ 08543-2053, (609) 452-1128.

Videos - Age

<u>Age Discrimination</u>. Available from Films for the Humanities & Sciences, P.O. Box 2053, Princeton, NJ 08543-2053, (609) 452-1128.